Helping
in the
Hallways

Second Edition

Helping
in the
Hallways

Second Edition

Expanding Your Influence Potential

Richard J. Hazler

CORWIN PRESS
A SAGE Company
Thousand Oaks, CA 91320

For information:

Corwin Press
A SAGE Company
2455 Teller Road
  Thousand Oaks,
    California 91320
www.corwinpress.com

SAGE India Pvt. Ltd.
B 1/I 1 Mohan Cooperative
  Industrial Area
Mathura Road, New Delhi 110 044
India

SAGE Ltd.
1 Oliver's Yard
55 City Road
London EC1Y 1SP
United Kingdom

SAGE Asia-Pacific Pte. Ltd.
33 Pekin Street #02-01
Far East Square
Singapore 048763

Printed in the United States of America.

Library of Congress Cataloging-in-Publication Data

Hazler, Richard J.
Helping in the hallways : expanding your influence potential/Richard J. Hazler. 2nd ed.
    p. cm.
1st ed. had a different subtitle.
Includes bibliographical references and index.
ISBN 978-1-4129-5607-9 (cloth : alk. paper)
ISBN 978-1-4129-5608-6 (pbk. : alk. paper)
    1. Educational counseling—United States. 2. Student counselors—United States. 3. Interpersonal relations—United States. 4. School discipline—United States. 5. Schools—United States—Safety measures. I. Title.

LB1027.5.H385 2008
371.7′8—dc22   2008001265

This book is printed on acid-free paper.

08 09 10 11 12 10 9 8 7 6 5 4 3 2 1

Acquisitions Editor:	Stacy Wagner
Managing Editor:	Jessica Allan
Editorial Assistant:	Joanna Coelho
Production Editor:	Eric Garner
Copy Editor:	Dorothy Hoffman
Typesetter:	C&M Digitals (P) Ltd.
Proofreader:	Charlotte J. Waisner
Indexer:	Ellen Slavitz
Graphic Designer:	Lisa Miller

Contents

Acknowledgments

Two superintendents in rural Idaho joined forces to hire a newly graduated school counselor to create the first counseling programs for both districts. Why they took a chance on an East Coast outsider after only telephone interviews has never been fully answered. But Florin Hulse (Murtaugh) and Percy Christensen (Hansen) did exactly that and allowed me to learn firsthand about getting the most value out of a school counseling position. We learned together about helping in the hallways, and for that I am forever grateful.

So many counselors, teachers, parents, administrators, and students have been among my greatest teachers over the years that I could not name them all. This educational community has provided the exquisite mixture of joys, tears, excitement, frustration, and support that has helped me see how important the diversity of people and ideas is to understanding and accepting others and myself.

—Richard J. Hazler

Corwin Press gratefully acknowledges the following peer reviewers for their editorial insight and guidance:

Becky Brannock, PhD, LPC
Professor
School Counseling Program Coordinator
Department of Psychology & Counseling
Pittsburg State University
Pittsburg, KS

Mary Ann Clark, PhD
Associate Professor and School Counseling Program
    Coordinator
Department of Counselor Education
University of Florida
Gainesville, FL

John P. Galassi
Professor, School Counseling, School of Education
The University of North Carolina at Chapel Hill
Chapel Hill, NC

Eric N. Jones
Principal
Elkhardt Middle School
Richmond Public Schools
Richmond, VA

Antanas "Tony" Levinskas, PhD, NCSP
Faculty, School Psychology
Harold Abel School of Psychology
Capella University
Minneapolis, MN

Paul B. Pedersen
Professor Emeritus
Syracuse University
Syracuse, NY
Visiting Professor University of Hawaii
Department of Psychology

Tod L. Petit
Elementary School Counselor
Ontario Local School District
Mansfield, OH

About the Author

**Richard J. Hazler** is Professor of Counselor Education at Penn State University in State College, Pennsylvania. He did graduate work at The College of New Jersey, and earned a PhD at the University of Idaho. He has worked as a school counselor and also as a counselor in the military, universities, a prison, and private practice. In addition, he has been an elementary school teacher, writer, and director of a variety of programs for young people. His research and writing includes numerous articles and books on a variety of topics, including bullying and victimization in schools, and the human side of counselors and educators. His most recent books include *The Emerging Professional Counselor: Student Dreams to Professional Realities* (2005), *Breaking the Cycle of Violence: Interventions for Bullying and Victimization* (1996), and *What You Didn't Learn in Graduate School: A Survival Guide for Therapists* (1997).

1

Life in the Hallways

FIVE-MINUTE ENLIGHTENING

It was my second year as the only school counselor for two small school districts in southern Idaho. The first year had been a good one, and people were happy with my work. Being the first school counselor either district had ever hired made everything new and challenging, and people were grateful for everything I did. But even with the success there were feelings of frustration. I was making a difference with some students, but most seemed out of reach. Plenty of credit was coming my way for counseling students, scheduling, records management, letters of reference, standardized testing, and other organizational activities, but that hardly made a dent in the needs of the majority of students and the school as a whole.

The students I saw were either very conniving at getting out of class or they were the worst problems who the teachers wanted out of class anyway. I felt isolated in the office, controlled by my environment, depressed, and I was thinking about looking for another job. There was just too much to do and no way I could see to make the impact I wanted.

One day, in the midst of what was becoming a regular state of depression, a teacher left a note asking to see me between periods. I never got to the teacher during my first try that day. A basketball player stopped me to say, "Great game last night, wasn't it? It meant a lot to see you out there supporting us." Another student I had never met asked about taking the ACT test. I patted a shy boy on the back just walking by and got a great smile for some contact we both appreciated. A new student waved for my attention asking if I would talk with her first-grade sister who was still frightened about coming to her new school. I was feeling important, cared about, and successful.

Nearly out of time to connect with the teacher between classes, I encountered more distractions. Two older boys seemed to be threatening a smaller boy, so I casually walked near, but not toward them, to draw their attention away from the brewing problem. It worked and they all moved on as I gave them a smile. One last approach by a student council member, who wanted to know if I could help with a problem the students were having with the principal, finally ended any possibility of seeing the teacher.

This one five-minute break between periods gave me more productive contact with more students than I had experienced the rest of the morning. All my best tools and training were put to use in these brief interactions. I listened, observed, gained understanding, provided support, modeled positive behaviors, offered quality advice when asked, and actually got invited into problems and issues that seemed critical to both individuals and the whole school. Even more important that particular day was the positive feedback I received about my work and myself. It was more than I had felt in a month! There was clearly something here that had been missing, and I wanted more of it on a daily basis.

This was not my first experience with being productive in the hallways of schools, playgrounds, and businesses; but never had I personally needed it more or recognized it so clearly. Perhaps that is why this one situation sticks with me and why the concepts of hallway helping have become so important to me. The counseling office is a wonderful place where great individual progress can be made. I love that work, but have come to realize that it has its limitations because it is also work in isolation. In order to have the larger influence on the school and community that is promoted by the American School Counselor Association and other entities it takes much more. Expanding that influence demands multiple brief, challenging, and supportive contacts. These are the contacts that take place in hallways, streets, athletic fields, playgrounds, lunchrooms, coffee shops, and teacher's rooms and at community events and anywhere else that people live their everyday lives. These are the places that put us in closer touch with the realities of students, faculty, administrators, parents, and even ourselves.

HALLWAY HEALTH

The term *hallways* is a metaphor for time spent outside the formal and structured offices and classrooms that tend to define our official roles. It certainly relates to the hallways in schools, but has come to mean much more than that. The hallways metaphor can be any of those places where people go about their daily lives in multiple ways. They are the places where individuals and groups feel more freedom to choose what they do rather than following more formal behavior guidelines. Here they also receive feedback that is more about who they are as persons rather than who they are as teachers, administrators, staff members, or students. These are places in which we connect directly with the true human realities of individuals and groups in ways that can be supportive of everyone involved.

The ability to maintain a positive sense of who you are and the life you lead is generally thought to come from satisfying the needs of autonomy, competence, and relatedness (Ryan & Deci, 2000). Opportunities to meet these needs can be found in places where personal growth, meaningful relationships, and connections to a community are available to promote a sense of well-being (Kasser & Ryan, 1996). These ingredients cannot be created in isolation, but instead require a social context with a diversity of people to both support who we are and encourage new growth. The greater diversity of groups with whom we interact and the wider variety of environments in which we participate, the greater is our potential for developing healthier and more productive perspectives on people, communities, and ourselves. We get better at helping and teaching as we gain greater connections to the fullness of people's lives.

> *The full diversity of people, ideas, and environments needed for maximum understanding and growth can be found only in the hallways of life, while professional spaces offer only highly selective and limited life exposures.*

Outside the classroom or office is where the most diverse groups of people meet in their natural environments. These are the places where people have greater freedom to make connections, meet personal needs, and develop relationships. They are the times and places in which we can help others while also meeting some of our own autonomy, competence, and relatedness needs. It is this type of environment where professionals have the greatest opportunity to feel integrated and connected to a community that can ward off the isolation from a diversity of people and ideas that are primary factors in professional burnout (Ghorpade, Lackritz, & Singh, 2007). Expanding our world outside of the office and classroom is good not only for those we serve, but for ourselves as well.

JOYS, RISKS, AND VALUE

What are the experiences counselors and educators remember? Many times they speak of the personal joys that they feel.

"At halftime of a basketball game a woman came up to me just to say thank you for helping her son. Her son had been explaining to her how he was making new friends since I introduced him to another student who I thought he'd like. It was a great feeling for me and I must admit that I liked others around us hearing it."

"It just feels natural and pleasant to be with the kids in the hallways where I can get smile after smile when I give one first. When you are dealing with problems so often, this is just a simple feel good for me."

But it is not always a pleasure to be in the hallways. Being in a natural and less-controlled environment means things can go in less than the best directions. There are risks in the hallways.

"Two teachers were arguing with each other in the teacher's room when I tried to step into the conversation and change it. Wrong thing to do! They told me in no uncertain terms to butt out! They didn't need my help. I was embarrassed and avoided them for two days."

"I stepped between two boys fighting and got a broken arm. Maybe not the right thing for a 5 foot 100 pound woman to do?"

It is not all about good and bad feelings gained in the hallways. Doing your job well and adding value to your services that couldn't be achieved within the limitations of the more formal professional environments is a major benefit.

"When I got a number of students involved in the local Kid's Day Celebration in the downtown area for the first time last year some really great things happened. Several of the middle school students who agreed to work with me were having behavior and academic problems.

(Continued)

(Continued)

Teaching younger kids and their parents how to do face painting all day gave them a new sense of pride in themselves, got them baby sitting jobs, and things started happening positively for them."

"I was asked to help coach the high school volleyball team and the relationships developed there really added to other aspects of my work. I learned so many things about what was really going on with kids from these relationships that I wouldn't get anywhere else. Not only that, but often the players would ask if there was some way they could help with individuals in need. I was gaining counseling supporters and tutors for other students from a place I'd never have expected."

There are many simple joys to be gained in the hallways that will keep your professional and personal strength and endurance up. It can change the professional educator's work from tiring to exhilarating and even relaxing at times. This type of work also adds value to our efforts to support the psychological, academic, and career development of youth in ways that can't be accomplished in more formal roles and situations. But although hallway helping is less formal, it does require professional skills and knowledge to make it work, because many more risks are involved when you leave more formal structures. Much of the remainder of this book is devoted to providing ideas and guidelines for interacting professionally within the less formal structure of hallway interactions.

Joys Felt	Risks Taken	Value Added
1. Being cared about	1. Rejection	1. Personal connections
2. Support	2. Looking foolish	2. Greater understanding
3. Sense of community	3. Biases	3. Self-understanding
4. Acceptance	4. Doing too much or too little	4. More ways to help

Joys Felt	Risks Taken	Value Added
5. Confirming success 6. Feeling connected 7. Learning 8. Simple pleasures 9. Relaxation 10. Pride	5. Overextending yourself 6. Abuse 7. Ineffectiveness 8. More mistake opportunities 9. Demonstrating lack of understanding 10. Stress of the unknown and unexpected	5. Breaking down barriers 6. Increasing communication 7. Demonstrating commitment 8. Becoming more integral to the community 9. Wider recognition 10. Acquiring helpers

LEARNING CLIMATE

Hallway helping cannot provide the in-depth guidance or extensive counseling that could be done in an office. It offers inadequate time and control to communicate the extended lessons and remediation that a classroom setting can provide. What it can do is proactively support these more intensive efforts through the development of a positive climate for personal, academic, social, and career growth that all students need.

Research has shown us how positive interpersonal relationships and optimal learning opportunities for students provide the atmosphere where achievement levels are higher while fewer behavioral and emotional problems arise (Kuperminc, Leadbeater, Emmons, & Blatt, 1997; McEvoy & Welker, 2000). Results around other issues often only hold true for white middle-class schools, but in the case of school climate, similar results can also be found in high-risk urban environments where positive, supportive, and culturally conscious school climates are maintained (Haynes & Comer, 1993).

The more positive supportive and culturally conscious relationships people build within a school, the greater will be academic learning within a safer, more secure, and more motivation conducive environment.

These benefits are not for students alone. Teachers, administrators, and other school professionals report increased job satisfaction with more positive school climates (Taylor & Tashakkori, 1995). When people feel more job satisfaction, they work harder to support colleagues and those they serve, making the outcome mutually beneficial for school professionals and students. We work better when we like where we are working.

Schools don't exist in a student and staff vacuum. Parents and the community also play vital roles in promoting learning, behavior, and racial socialization in schools (Henderson & Berla, 1994; McKay, Atkins, Hawkins, Brown, & Lynn, 2003). This is a two-way street; a climate conducive of their involvement is necessary to gain the benefits of positive parent involvement in the schools. One difficulty is that parents don't spend day after day attending school under the rules and expectation designed for students. We must find other methods and places to help them see schools as an appropriate ally and that requires being proactive about supporting and investing in them. We need to meet them not just in our territory (school), but also in the hallways of their lives, which will primarily be outside of the school.

The hallways of life for everyone in a community are important ingredients in developing a productive and supportive environment for students. Reaching out to individuals and groups is the only way to develop such wide connections. Current school practices set those kind of broad community-building goals for us, but how we go about it depends on recognizing the unique aspects of ourselves that influence thinking and reactions to hallway life.

EXPANDING INFLUENCE AND IDEAS

This second edition of *Helping in the Hallways* has expanded its scope and size in reaction to the ever-increasing demands on counselors, teachers, and all school staff. No longer can those involved in education operate in relative isolation from others.

An increasingly diverse and education-demanding society requires all educators to practice extensive cooperation and collaboration to achieve success for students of every ability level and cultural variety. These pressures have guided many changes in this edition, including the diversity of examples and activities appropriate for use by teachers, administrators, and all educators in addition to counselors.

Many revisions and additions reflect the emphasis on seeing to it that all students achieve the academic, career, and social success identified in publications such as the *ASCA Model* and in the No Child Left Behind legislation. Criticism of these efforts has often centered on how potential rigidity and impersonal implementation can lead to additional problems instead of the desired success. Expanded hallway activities, experiences, and reasoning are used to show how professionals can support the more formal aspects of these efforts and produce the vital personal motivation for students and adults involved in the process.

Changes in this second edition have also evolved from professionals in the field who have offered experiences and perspectives in reaction to the first edition. Readers will therefore see additional activities from my own experiences and those of other school professionals. Their feedback also communicated a desire to see important aspects summarized and emphasized in more visual ways. This guidance is reflected in some format changes including additional tables and borders that better highlight and summarize key points, activities, and experiences.

FINDING YOUR WAY IN THE HALLWAYS

There is no one right way to get all the benefits from the hallways. It always involves interactions between the type of person you are, the people with whom you will be interacting, and the context of the situation. Classrooms and offices add controls to limit the variables that need to be taken into account. Imagine a counseling office with a desk in the middle of the lunchroom or a writing class that was held outdoors every day, regardless of the weather. No one would suggest such arrangements because they increase the variables that would get in the way of accomplishing the desired task. But hallway interactions locate themselves in such areas where we have less control, more variables to consider, and importantly, more information available for learning and helping. The task is to become increasingly proficient at understanding the varied nature of hallway environments and identifying the actions that fit best.

The first three chapters are an orientation to hallway helping and how changing pressures require new models for education and educators. The inherent value in the hallways and beyond that isn't available in more controlled environments has increasing importance as more and different accomplishments are expected from counselors, teachers, staff, administrators, and parents. These factors increase the potential value of hallway helping that begins with the ability to assess how to make hallway helping work best for your style and situation.

Understanding the needs and how you relate to them in your work is followed in the second section, with an emphasis on understanding the process of helping in the hallways. It is a process with a common form that is implemented differently for various groups. Unique aspects of students, teachers, staff, administrators, and parents need to be taken into account while implementing the process and the specific actions within the process.

The variety of possible hallway actions is limited only by your creativity and energy. The final section provides a bank of hallway activities to get your creative thinking started. Some come from my professional school experience while others come from professionals who have reported positive results. See which ones fit your situations, and try them out or adapt them to meet your specific needs. Enjoy the process and you will find others enjoying and learning from it as well.

2

Hallway Challenges

The realities of student life are not found in classrooms and offices. It is in the hallways and on the playgrounds that kindergartners first get lost and scared only to later develop confidence as they find their way around. It is here that bigger kids try pushing others around until someone or something stops them. Smaller kids gain confidence by learning how to hold onto seats on the bus or places in line. Some children are blessed with invitations into a group and others are shunned. Threats, punishments, praise, and plans can all be parts of quick trips to the restroom. Tears over College Board exams and plans to get a car for the dance are played out in school parking lots and local hangouts.

The illusion of a sanitized academic life that we fabricate in our classrooms and counseling offices is stripped away in the hallways. What remains are the best and worst of real life. Our training and commitment as counselors and educators is sorely needed in this hallway world, but our training has not focused on how to make the greatest impact there.

A trip through the hallways is no simple excursion for professionals. Problems, confusion, sorrows, frustrations, and anxieties are there for anyone who wants to help. Attend to them and you can make a difference. Duck out of the way, and you have done much less than is possible.

There are also a wealth of pleasures, excitement, fun, and accomplishments waiting to be recognized and enjoyed in the hallways. Your simple presence, a smile of recognition, a pat on the back, or an offer of support can do wonders for students and for yourself. But forget to congratulate someone on her newest source of pride or fail to recognize a meekly waved hello, and you can be seen as just another uncaring adult.

Rules are less clear once you get outside school offices and classrooms, which makes the risks higher, but also creates opportunities. Circumstances outside the classroom offer more freedom to act on life's realities and the chance for immediate impact that is not available in more formal environments.

What problems make hallways more challenging today? What can schools and communities do to strengthen the best that hallways have to offer and minimize their inherent problems? How can counselors and educators of all types make the most of these situations with the professional skills they already have and in the limited time available? Heaven knows you have more than enough to do already, and another book should not add to that burden. Instead, what is needed to deal with the daily challenges to be faced are interventions that take comparatively little time or planning and reap new rewards for everyone, including you.

CHANGING PRESSURES

A teacher once tried to summarize the changes she saw when she recently retired with 35 years of experience as a teacher and school counselor.

"It began as a relationship between a class of junior high students and me. I learned about them and they learned the material to different degrees that seemed to mostly match their abilities and interests. The

> relationships were the most exciting parts of the teaching, which was the motivator to become a school counselor where, for a number of years, I mainly counseled individuals and groups while also teaching some guidance lessons. But things began changing with more concerns about school violence, learning problems, the No Child Left Behind legislation, and testing, testing, testing. There was more and more to do with little guidance as to how to get them all done.
>
> The ASCA Model at least provided a comprehensive focus and order to deal with the increasing tensions felt by students, teachers, administrators, and parents. The sad part of these last few years was how little emphasis relationships seemed to be given by outside forces in comparison to achievement. Those of us inside schools knew how important relationships were in the learning and growing process and we did all we could to develop them. But unlike my first years, it had become a continuing battle to find the time and new ways to promote relationships."

It seems that everyone in education is being asked to do more with less even as the problems we deal with change. Professionals today have widely different challenges to deal with than they did in 1940 when teachers rated their top disciplinary problems as talking out of turn, chewing gum, making noise, running in the hall, cutting in line, and questioning dress code rules. Fifty years later, those problems might seem like the discipline concerns of a model school. Now we face responsibility for prevention, intervention, and remediation of people and situations that elicit greater concerns about violence and dangerous consequences. In the 1990s, teachers identified problems they face as assault, robbery, drug abuse, pregnancy, and suicide (Toch, 1993).

Academic issues made up the bulk of the National Education Goals 2000, which were reinforced by the 2001 No Child Left Behind Act. The U.S. Department of Education (2006) pointed to National Assessment of Educational Progress results showing improved student achievement in reading and math while also helping to close the achievement gap between minority and white students. Critics focused on issues of inadequate funding, narrow curriculum, and research being too limited to specific forms of testing (McKenzie, 2003). These heavy reading- and math-focused initiatives have clearly produced some gains, but they have come at a cost of reduced emphasis and time spent on social and physical development through the arts, social understanding, and physical education.

Creating safe, disciplined, and drug-free schools was one of six key goals identified in the 1993 National Education Goals Panel. The panel's 1996 follow-up report did not bode well for reaching those goals any time in the near future. Drug use and drug sales on school grounds were up; alcohol use had stayed the same; 30% more teachers reported being threatened in school; and discipline problems were increasingly interfering with instruction.

The goals of making schools safe, disciplined, and drug-free environments where everyone is academically and socially successful are laudable for sure. Unfortunately, they often come as edicts that print up very nicely, but ignore the human requirement for connections and community with others to reach a person's full potential.

> *Interpersonal improvements come from emphasizing relationships among everyone involved, not edicts, goals, and demands to change.*

Pressures created by the disequilibrium, tension, and high emotional levels found in schools can create havoc among individuals and groups. The most basic reaction to such pressures is to create increasingly more rules, harsher rules, and more cumulative consequences to those who break the rules. This model has provided for little success and greater harm in communities as diverse as schools and dictator-ruled nations. In fact, more stringent rules demand more active enforcement, which creates a whole new set of pressures on those with the least influence and quietest voices. Diversity of culture, thinking, and new ideas are sacrificed for the consistency demanded by those who hold power. Minorities become the most likely to be ignored in favor of the loud and powerful. The result is antagonistic and subversive reactions rather than the calming influence and cooperation that increased rule making was designed to promote.

The observations of several educational professionals on how rigid reactions to improving academic achievement and school safety highlight how the human need for relationship can get lost in the process:

> *"Teachers have a mandate to get those kids' scores up! All else is secondary. If you want relationships, then you have to find your own time for them."*
>
> *"Zero Tolerance is big here. Who cares whether the discipline citations were for carrying guns or dozing in class. The stricter we get, the more logic goes out the window."*
>
> *"Kids and adults are both stretched toward the limits of what they can handle. More paper and computer requirements with no more school time available, mean that more outside of school time is essential to satisfy the demands. Time in school may be no longer than it was, but hours needed to keep up with school requirements has stretched well beyond the normal school day."*

Other counselors at a recent conference expressed strong opinions on how various groups in the school were being affected by the increasing pressures:

> *"So many social concerns about race, gender, and social status have opened up for valuable discussion and growth for the whole community, but the demand for academic time-on-task seems to override what could be gained in these areas."*
>
> *"Students have so little time to thmselves that I see them having more trouble making good decisions. Requirements are more rigid in school, homework follows them away from school, and then so much of their play is even organized whether it is sports, dance, arts, or something else. Everything is training rather than play. Where is the fun and the time to explore life on your own?"*
>
> *(Continued)*

(Continued)

"Too many parents don't feel that the school is a place where they will be respected. Particularly those that are not in the social, cultural, or economic majority tend to stay away. They've had enough of people telling them what they need to do and not listening to them when they have something to say."

"The pressure to continually raise test scores has the teachers who care the most, frustrated at not being able to give them the full experience of what learning could be if they were freed from so many controls."

"Administrators are paid more money to be in charge, but even they complain of feeling like there are too many things to do with too few resources."

So who is benefiting from more tests, more rules, and stronger consequences? This is a good question without a solid answer for schools or society as a whole. Government is spending more on law enforcement, yet we feel less secure. We catch more people breaking an increasing number of laws, and then we put more of them behind bars for longer sentences. And still we feel less safe and have to pay more for police protection and prisons.

Reading and math scores appear to be rising with the increased emphasis given to them, although the jury is still out on the overall impact. Will better scores create more of the workers we need in the future? Perhaps, more important, will the added academic pressures create a better citizenry when the students become adults? Both questions arise out of the concern for how much social learning and personal development may be changed as more time is taken up by what adults require children to do and less time is available for making independent work, play, and relationship choices.

Research also tells us that simply creating more organization and making tougher rules is not the answer. Five-minute time-outs before children can get back to learning and making choices do as much good as 20-minute time-outs (McGuffin,

1991). Troubled families are another example where deterioration is generally accompanied by a pattern of creating more and harsher rules that have no positive effect. In fact, just the opposite occurs, as the increasing demands seem to pump up the pressures and speed up the decline (Miller & Prinz, 1990). It is clear that creating additional rules and increasing their level of enforcement alone will not create the students, schools, and society we desire.

Anger and frustration from developmental differences, unequal abilities, racial bias, sexual discrimination, socioeconomic prejudices, and power imbalances between groups and individuals cannot be legislated or punished away. Long-term hope for our schools and students lies in the quality of academic, professional, and personal relationships that caring professionals, students, and parents are willing to implement in real-world experiences.

MEETING CHALLENGES IN THE HALLWAYS

Getting the next generation of adults ready to be successful in an increasingly diverse and complex society is no easy task. The challenges are many, and we must take the best of what we know while also looking beyond traditional formal models to find new ways of making things work better. One key model found to be effective is diligent implementation of more personal involvement by professionals in shaping real-life relationships between everyone in a community. Taking time to demonstrate positive relationships in the hallways and streets where such relationships are not normally invited will produce beneficial changes and results we are all seeking. It is a proactive approach designed to improve the system, even when the focus is on one person or one group at a time.

Urban Success

Why does Browne Junior High in the middle of troubled Washington, D.C., have a history of academic success and an attendance rate of 92%? Credit is given to a principal who knows every student by name, a staff whose words and actions show pride and belief in their students. It is a school in which people are demonstrative and energetic and the parents know the staff because of their involvement in the community. The curriculum and school hours remain fairly consistent while the results have changed dramatically. It is outside the offices and classrooms where these differences are being made and positive relationships with members of the school community are being formed.

From Unruly to Model School

How did another Washington, D.C., junior high transform itself from an unruly school with massive discipline problems and poor attendance into a model school? Hine Junior High continued to have poor plumbing and bad security problems, but the atmosphere and actions of the students and staff changed dramatically, and they now can hold their heads high. The greatest amount of credit for the turnaround was given to the staff's increasing involvement with the hallway and street lives of their students, in addition to attending more closely to only "a few basic rules" that are understood and accepted by almost everyone.

Unity, Pride, and Hope Can Thrive

A Catholic elementary school for the arts exists in a crime-ridden neighborhood of the Bronx, New York, where 75% of the students come from one-parent families, 20% have one or more parents with a substance abuse problem, and 30% live on public assistance. Why is this school thriving with unity, pride, hope, and success, even after fire destroyed two-thirds of their main building? One student summed up the feelings of many: "The teachers care about us. They want us to succeed, to go on in life." A mother put it another way: "It wouldn't matter if the classes were in the alley. It's the spirit of the place that counts for kids in this kind of community."

Tapping Positive Relationship Potential

What do these success stories have in common? It was not loads of money, the elimination of poverty, the eradication of prejudice, or continual development of newer and stricter rules that made the difference. The professionals in these schools are moving outside their offices and classrooms to tap the positive potential of more casual relationships within their schools and communities. School counselors and other dedicated professionals are right in the middle of initiating this growth and making it work.

These schools are places where kids like to be and where the professionals are feeling better about their work than they have in years. These schools and others were not always like this. It takes energy and a new way of looking at the educational experience to make the necessary system and individual changes. No matter how good change sounds, there is always a natural resistance to change under even the best of circumstances.

When people have figured out how to do a job with some degree of success, it is no easy step to move into uncharted waters. What overcomes the resistance, encourages and solidifies these risky steps are the benefits that come with the more personalized interactions and camaraderie. School becomes a place where you can both find support for yourself and give it as needed to face the challenges we all meet in life. These are schools where a few key people begin to consistently exemplify to everyone the hallway characteristics of joy, excitement, hope, support, and adventure. Others follow later, as they begin to see on a daily basis how the new approach can directly improve their lives.

These positive interpersonal relationships are directly reflected in the characteristics of safer and more effective schools that are generally smaller and/or actively promote cohort relationships. It is this greater access to quality relationships that allows people to meet each other, develop understanding, and increase their sources of support and new information. We expand our knowledge and understanding of people and the world through the additional diversity of cultures, beliefs, skills, and worldviews. Classrooms become well disciplined when the positive aspects of relationships can be more fully explored. These are the schools where students, faculty, and parents all recognize and appreciate a connectedness between the classroom, the hallways, and the neighborhood.

Students in safer and more effective schools truly believe the staff encourages them to have a significant influence on the life of the school as opposed to feeling their lives are run by others. This research seems to suggest what real-life examples confirm:

> *Individual staff members who add most to a healthy school environment are those who persistently initiate opportunities for quality relationships outside their offices and classrooms.*

School counselors and other mental health professionals stand out as the individuals with the most direct training to initiate and support these efforts. They have the potential to be leaders in the movement, but the human potential is also there for other professionals and parents alike to create the improved relationships that can strengthen our schools and all those involved in them.

ASCA COLLABORATIVE MODEL

Collaborative effort is a key ingredient in all the positive effects on school performance. Professionals or parents working in isolation may benefit individual students, but that work doesn't directly impact others or the overall school. It takes a broader approach to the school and the diversity of human potential involved to produce the broader impact desired.

The American School Counselor Association (ASCA) has provided leadership for counselors and others on how to achieve such collaborative efforts and a broad focus on all students. The ASCA National Model (Bowers & Hatch, 2005) focuses on the work of the school counselor, but the directions and messages apply to everyone desiring to influence learning and schools. They emphasize working with all the critical aspects of students that will promote success during and after formal schooling. It is a model that recognizes the importance of working with everyone in the schools, parents, and community to acquire measurable success.

The ASCA Model gives particular importance to achievement in the three domains of Academic Development, Career Development, and Personal/Social Development. Emphasis is given to each area, recognizing that success in any one area is influenced by the others. These are the same student achievement components that can be found in successful schools supported by the concepts, processes, and techniques of hallway helping.

Hallway helping is a supportive aspect of the ASCA Model's overall efforts needed to support the success of all students in schools. Helping in the hallways touches all the model areas, but is not the primary vehicle for providing services. The model emphasizes formal guidance services, individual student planning, responsive services, and systems support, most of which take place in formal spaces such as offices and classrooms. Hallway helping provides the informal follow-up actions designed to reinforce information, attitudes, and skills. These actions take place in less formal settings where everyday aspects of life can be integrated into learning and experimentation on new information, attitudes, and behaviors can take place.

MAKING THE HALLWAYS WORK FOR YOU

Those who want to improve school safety, morale, and achievement through a hallways approach need to ask themselves some hard personal questions to judge their potential for success. Professionals are already leading busy lives with more than enough work to do. Money and awards will not come flowing to you if you attend more to hallway interactions. There are plenty of reasons why each of us would resist changing the ways we work, and there is probably little official demand to fight that resistance. Before we look at all the things we might do differently, it is important to think about those factors that might make us hesitate, the factors that would move us to change, and the ways they interact to produce the choices we make. We have the mission and the skills to promote positive relationships among students, teachers, parents, administrators, and the community, but there are also natural pressures that force us to make some difficult choices on what roles to take and when to take them.

Speaking Up

The challenge is to recognize and use the informal power available to you in order to make use of all your potential influence. It is often easier to keep your mouth shut and back away than to speak out or act in difficult situations. The problem with keeping quiet is that you may wind up following someone else's bad directions. Your quality professional voice needs to be heard.

Taking Risks

Positive change and growth are available in the confusing, uncertain crowds outside the office and classroom, but they also force you to relinquish some security. Risk is firmly attached to the importance of what you do and the satisfaction you find. Some will take the safer, more stable routes by making limited choices, acting in more rigid ways, and minimizing change. But the stability this creates eventually turns into boredom and dull sameness as the many burned-out professionals who seek therapy or leave the profession can attest. Some degree of risk taking is essential to stimulate enthusiasm and excitement.

Stepping Out

What a joy it was as neophyte professionals to walk into new rooms, arrange pencils, store pads, put up thoughtful decorations, and align the seats just right. We naively expected the most amazing things would happen on an hourly basis. It didn't take long before we realized how many critical relationships were going on outside these carefully ordered spaces and that people usually take their problems and needs to someone else. These are the times when you choose between shrinking back to deal with as few people and tasks as possible and stepping out to develop new personal and professional relationships in unfamiliar territory.

Diversity Immersion

Growth comes from new information and new experiences with people and cultures. All life maintains itself over time by diversification. Plants, animals, or human beings cannot survive with only one variety. Individual people have differences and cultures vary around race, gender, languages, and styles of living. The less diversity you open yourself to, the less you can learn and consequently the less help you can be to others. Helping in the hallways requires immersing oneself in the culture of those that are not in your traditional circle of friends, colleagues, and acquaintances. You need to meet those not like you on their grounds rather than your own.

Leading the Advance

Professional training, skills, and access to students and staff put you in a position to take a leadership role. The mantle of leadership cannot be avoided forever if you are to make the most of your talents. Sometimes leadership is desired, other times it is thrust on us, and occasionally we take it because there is no other acceptable alternative. The variable pressures to be follower, leader, and even hermit are what we must recognize as part of just being human. Facing the choices and making the most of our abilities is what brings us the most pride in ourselves and the work we do.

There are no ultimate right and wrong choices about how each of us becomes an initiator of better things for our students and schools, but the location for vibrant, new, possible actions is clear:

> *Reality, opportunity for change, human variety, and challenge are greatest in the hallways, playgrounds, parking lots, and streets where people are actively moving through their lives.*

Knowing Yourself

Just as a piano does not have a single best key or combination of keys, neither do you have one way that will always work best. The secret is in knowing as many keys and combinations as possible so that you can continually experiment with developing better and more pleasing patterns of relationships. Even the people who are as different as the sharps and flats on a piano can be arranged in the right combination with the right timing to make a positive human symphony.

The remainder of this book provides new relationship development strategies and shows you how to use some old skills in new ways. Whether you use the whole model or separate pieces to create your own personal style of helping is up to you. Either way can change the patterns of your work to better encourage a healthier environment in and around the hallways of your school.

The success someone finds in hallways techniques will be a combination of his or her personal style, the other(s) involved, the situation, and the techniques that combine them best. The starting place is to know oneself, so the following are good questions to begin thinking about yourself or someone you want to encourage to take on more hallway interactions. Follow the directions to help identify the changes that seem most valuable to you and also those on which you are most ready to try something new.

My Motivation for Hallways Change

Circle the answer that best fits you at this time.

1. How comfortable am I with the way things are with my current work?

    1 = Not at all   2 = Relatively comfortable 3 = I like it the way it is

2. How much would I like to improve the climate of the school?

    1 = It is fine   2 = Some change needed   3 = Lots of change needed

3. How willing am I to step into cultures with values very different from mine?

    1 = Not willing   2 = Somewhat willing   3 = Looking forward to it

4. Do I want more relationship connections with students or less?

    1 = Less   2 = Okay as is   3 = More

5. Do I want increased relationships with colleagues or less?

    1 = Less   2 = Okay as is   3 = More

6. Do I want closer connections to administrators or less?

    1 = Less   2 = Okay as is   3 = More

7. Do I want more connections with staff or less?

    1 = Less   2 = Okay as is   3 = More

8. Do I want more involvement with parents or less?

    1 = Less   2 = Okay as is   3 = More

9. Do I want more connections in the community or less?

    1 = Less   2 = Okay as is   3 = More

(Continued)

(Continued)

10. How ready am I to speak up for what I want in productive ways?

    1 = Not ready   2 = Somewhat ready   3 = Very ready

11. How much risk am I willing to take to make the changes I'd like to see?

    1 = Very little   2 = Conservative risk   3 = A lot

12. How much anxiety do I have about stepping into less structured environments?

    1 = A lot   2 = Some   3 = Little

13. How much am I willing to be a leader of change?

    1 = None   2 = Significant change   3 = Lots of change

What are you willing to change?_____

_____

Total score for 13 items to assess general readiness for change

    13–21 = Hesitant about making hallway changes in general
    22–30 = Reasonably ready for hallway changes in general
    31–39 = Very much ready to make hallway changes in general

What *specific changes do you feel are most valuable and you feel ready to change?*

    1 _____   5 _____
    2 _____   6 _____
    3 _____   7 _____
    4 _____   8 _____

3

Evaluating Hallway Relationships

Parents know to follow the sign at the entry to every school: "Please report directly to the principal's office." When students are in class, the hallways are deceptively quiet and peaceful places. Then the bell rings, and the quiet corridors turn into a turmoil where parents caught out in the open hug the walls for safety. Neither the chaos and confusion of students jostling in the halls nor the deceptive serenity when they are in the classroom conveys much about the people involved. It is the individual experiences of joy, safety, anxiety, and danger that are at the heart of hallway experiences. Consider just a few of examples that professionals know all too well.

- *At the high school, Gwenn is pregnant and hasn't told anyone.*
- *Ms. Navarro, the new middle school principal, inherited a good school by all accounts, but there are bullying issues and racial differences in standardized test scores that deserve attention if the school is to continue to improve.*

- *Pushing, shoving, and cursing get Dan in trouble daily when he leaves his fourth-grade classroom. Mr. Bandu is angry because he gets questioned about what happens in his class that has Dan coming out of it so inappropriately?*
- *Dwan thinks the world will collapse if he doesn't get into the "right" college.*
- *The PTA president had a heart attack at a critical time, and the extremely shy vice president would rather quit than take the job, so she asks you to fix things for her.*

The realities of people's lives in the hallways would make the strongest professionals want to run away and hide, and sometimes that is just what we do.

SECURITY SPACES

There is no place where I can do counseling as effectively as in my office. It provides security, isolation, time, confidentiality, structure, and control that are available nowhere else with such consistency. A good office is the perfect place for standard counseling and administrative work, a setting in which you can create a controlled detachment from the confusion of the rest of the world. But sometimes that detachment is not so controlled, and the office can become a means of escape.

Teachers report much the same feelings about their classrooms where organization and control allow for the effective use of lesson plans. Administrators also appreciate the quiet of an office to conduct business. Other staff may or may not have offices, but they do have work locations that serve similar purposes. All these situations provide an environmental continuity in ways that allow people to plan for carrying out their jobs with a minimum of distractions.

As effective as the office or classroom can be, it can also be used addictively as a hiding place where life outside can be avoided. The signs of hallway avoidance may be as simple as the sinking feeling in your stomach, the increased pounding of your heart, or the deep sigh that comes when you prepare to leave the office. Perhaps it is the unexpected desire to make one more telephone call, score one more test, fill out one more form, or write one more letter of reference. As frustrating as administrative duties can be, they can also offer relief from dealing with more difficult problems waiting outside.

As with any addiction, some people continuously give in to the relief opportunities and leave the real world behind as often as possible. Others reject the avoidance urge altogether and forgo important tasks to stay in the middle of hallway turmoil continuously. Most find ways to blend periods of security in their assigned space with hallway turmoil in order to maintain a measure of control while still facing hallway realities on a regular basis.

Finding the time and energy to use and enjoy hallway relationships requires a simple, yet flexible plan to guide your efforts and provide opportunities for greater control when things go awry. The starting place is to determine the essential pieces of information needed to quickly decide on appropriate actions. You have already proven your interpersonal skills, so this plan should put you in a position to implement those skills quickly, in more places, more often. Start by identifying your goals and limitations.

LIMITED TIME = LIMITED GOALS

Hallway helping does not have the luxury of extended controlled time periods that a counseling office or classroom can offer. What you can do in one to five minutes in a crowd is not what you can do for a half hour or hour in your official space. Other opportunities like extracurricular activities or community activities might give you more time with a person, but less opportunity to deal with important issues. To be successful in hallway helping, your actions will have to reflect the limitations of this approach while emphasizing its unique strengths.

Working out the details of difficult situations, taking an in-depth look at oneself, walking through a decision-making process, and doing extensive problem solving are not goals for hallway interactions. The time and confidentiality needed for these demanding goals are best found in a formal private space.

Hallway goals fill in the practical gaps for these larger goals by developing productive relationships; recognizing when one is in a difficult situation; verifying times when a new understanding of one's self is demonstrated; providing immediate support for a good decision or recognition that another decision didn't work; and encouraging the practice of problem-solving techniques in the real world.

> *Hallway helping at its best provides for the numerous brief interactions needed to reinforce positive happenings in a person's life and to communicate short bursts of support when people need a lift. The goal is to provide personalized and targeted interactions as regularly as possible to as many people as possible.*

Chaos theory tells us that even the smallest, seemingly insignificant actions, when combined with other factors in a person's environment, can turn out to make a greater difference over time than any one major directed action. The essence of hallway helping is continuously making small differences in peoples' lives through reminding, attending, and reality recognition. The long-term life goals are still important, but they must involve smaller, incremental steps.

> *It is better to take many small steps in the right direction than to make a great leap forward only to stumble backward.* (Old Chinese Proverb)

The hallway helper must focus on smaller goals and the related steps in order to recognize the value of their interactions and the progress being made. Limitations associated with these goals make it imperative that the hallway helper focus attention on the key factors about a person and her or his situation so that helpful actions can be taken as quickly and as frequently as possible. The following are questions to consider next:

- How ready is a person to change?
- How does the context of a problem influence how to proceed?
- When do you act faster or more slowly?
- How do you choose a location for a hallway interaction?

READINESS TO ACT

One of our greatest frustrations is seeing clearly what people need to do yet not being able to get them to act.

- *Dan wants to be liked, but his aggressive style turns others off and he doesn't accept his own role in the problem.*
- *Gwenn knows she needs to begin working things out with her mother and father as quickly as possible, but fear of what might happen is what she needs to overcome.*
- *Ms. Navarro sees the need for changes in teaching strategies, how teachers, staff, and students treat each other, and how to put greater emphasis on learning. Unfortunately, her style of approaching these issues with people is not helping.*

These cases display different degrees of readiness to work on issues, which affects what hallway, office, or classroom strategies might be most beneficial to each individual. How willing people are to work and the abilities they have to get the work done are the key readiness ingredients.

Willingness

The degree to which people have sufficient interpersonal motivation and confidence to succeed at a relationship task will determine their potential for an assertive approach and successful outcome. A lack of willingness results in no situation being small enough to handle, no idea easy enough to grasp, and no amount of ability sufficient for success. Too much willingness can lead to overconfidence that can result in a lack of preparation for decisions and actions. People who have the need and potential to make positive changes in their lives generally fall somewhere in the middle of a willingness continuum along which resistant behaviors are at one end, responsive behaviors are in the middle, and overconfident behaviors lie at the other extreme.

Resistant	*Responsive*	*Overconfident*

Resistant

High tension levels in a person can create opposition to taking action regardless of how valuable it might be. Educators are regularly frustrated by students, teachers, administrators, or parents who have the ability and need to learn something new or change their behaviors, but are resolutely unwilling to consider doing what is needed. A steady approach that does not drive the person away combined with patience are the keys to promoting quality growth when high tension levels and opposition are likely.

Responsive

Moderate tension levels tend to be good for motivating people to change. Anxiety is present in sufficient amounts to raise concerns, while still allowing movement toward action. This level of anxiety provides a push for people to act, but not such a hard push that they reject acting out of fear. These are among the most productive tension levels for helping, when people feel the need for assistance in their development and welcome potential helpers. The personal rewards for helpers are also great at this stage, when help is sought and appreciated.

Overconfident

Low tension levels combined with high confidence levels might sound like the perfect situation, but this is often not the case. When confidence is inappropriately high, preparation for taking action and the level of energy put into the action are often not sufficient to produce the desired results. Generally, overconfidence is connected to a lack of information or concern about oneself or a situation, so that anxiety is inappropriately low. People with needs at these levels are likely to either not act or act in ways that don't help themselves or their situation. This is one area where potential helpers need to find ways to actually raise anxiety to more realistic levels to spur effective actions.

Abilities

Whereas the willingness factor is the best determiner of whether a person is likely to begin or follow through with making changes, the information and skills someone brings to the task are what define the ability to carry the task out effectively. Only when people bring the necessary abilities to the task or can learn them during the process can both they and those who would help them experience feelings of success. For most purposes, you can decide that a person will be either "able" or "unable" to deal with the nature and difficulty level of a specific task at a given time. The degree and type of ability a person has or lacks are primary factors in determining when and in what ways to intervene.

Readiness Decisions

Willingness and ability factors combine to influence the ways in which you must act to be successful. The following are some ways that these factors might relate to the decisions regarding hallway actions to take with Dan, Gwenn, and Ms. Navarro:

- *A lack of ability in the area of social relationships is Dan's greatest problem. He would like to have better relationships with peers (willingness), but he doesn't have confidence in any of his skills other than to be inappropriately aggressive.*

Hallway interactions with Dan can focus on strengthening ability to change by modeling appropriate social skills, short-circuiting potentially inappropriate behaviors or difficult situations, and showing support for productive social behaviors.

- *Gwenn is at a moderate to high anxiety level of willingness (responsive) at which she is worried, but definitely recognizes the need to act. She has plenty of relationship skills (ability) to begin dealing with the situation and enough willingness to take initial actions. Encouragement, support, and reinforcement for Gwenn's decisions and actions would be the emphasis of hallway interactions.*

- *Ms. Navarro is perhaps more willing to act (overconfident) than she is prepared to act (ability). She doesn't seem to have a good sense of how her behaviors are negatively influencing staff and students so that she is losing support for her ideas rather than gaining the support she wants and needs. The first task will be to either find a way to gain Ms. Navarro's trust or gain the involvement of someone whom she does trust. Direct suggestions or recommendations on how she might act differently are likely to go unheard because of her current overconfidence. It will take someone trusted to help her see that less confidence, better understanding of the situation, and exploration of new ways to interact with staff and students will be more effective.*

Context Assessment

Recognizing the immediate situations of those you contact is an important early step on entering hallway relationships. Gwenn is young, unmarried, in school, and pregnant. How you deal with her issues should be far different from how you approach Dan's aggressiveness, the principal's concerns for the school, or the PTA vice president's shyness. What should influence the interventions you try are the personal, social, or academic nature of the situation as well as where, when, and how you interact. The faster you can match what you say and do to the other person's context, the more likely you will be to have a productive hallway relationship.

Personal Context

Students often need to interpersonally process thoughts, feelings, and choices before they share them with others or take direct action. This highly personal context requires clarification of needs, beliefs, desires, and goals that generally deserve the isolation and time provided in an office. Brief hallway interventions become more valuable as highly personal issues begin to display themselves in public arenas and take on a more social nature.

Gwenn's unwanted and unexpected pregnancy is a personal issue of major proportions. Exploring her feelings about it, considering her options, breaking the news to her parents, discussing possibilities with the father-to-be, and what it will mean to her life are critical personal issues that need to be discussed thoughtfully and in private. Only after she has her thoughts, emotions, and reasoning more firmly together will the hallways become appropriate for the more social context of work with parents, friends, and boyfriend.

Social Context

Many times, students understand what they need to do and already have the skills or ability to implement necessary changes. Problems in a social context involve students practicing in the real world and with real people what they know in their heads or can put into words, but have trouble implementing in real life. This is an ideal context for hallway helping.

Dan is bigger than the other kids, and his pushing and shoving make him feel powerful and in control. Talking to Dan in an office may not make the desired dent in his perceptions of how to deal with people or how they react to him. Short interventions with Dan outside the office have the advantage of directly attending to the issues of power and control in the actual social context where real people and real reactions are immediately available.

The PTA vice president provides a very different example of how the concept of hallway helping can be expanded beyond the literal hallways of schools. She is a mature and competent woman with hesitancies about being in the public eye. What she needs most is to practice her abilities by being encouraged, supported, and having her value recognized in public. Professionals who help her move into those situations with the necessary support provided both immediately and afterwards are the ones who can turn a seemingly unrelated situation into one that influences students, administrators, and parents throughout the community.

Academic Context

Many student, parent, and teacher issues relate to the professional or academic context of the school. This academic emphasis revolves around student reading, clarifying, relating, and recalling. They include discussions of scheduling, program planning, career exploration, and interviewing for work. These issues require that attention first be given to the person's formal role within the school community (student, counselor, teacher, administrator, committee member, etc.) with personal and social contexts temporarily given a secondary status.

Dwan wants desperately to get into a college as soon as possible. This need falls first into the academic context. Matching his student context with your role as knowledgeable and helpful professional can be easily done in the hallways and need not start in an extended private session. Casual comments and brief discussions can give Dwan much to think about, resources to find, direct actions to take, and things to talk about with others. Numerous informal interactions on a regular basis will increase the academic and personal bonds between the two of you as well as his knowledge base.

Ms. Navarro provides a different view of an academic context. She feels great pressure to increase test scores and decrease student bullying to be judged effective by the superintendent. Her personal pressures and anxieties will not be the ones she presents, however. She is more likely to be taking a strong stand on the academic and climate needs of the school rather than the personal reasons that are pushing her to dramatic actions.

Because she approaches the issues in an academic context, the best way to begin strengthening your influence with her is to match that context. Thoughtful listening to her frustrations with school personnel and students is the best starting place for a relationship that could become productive in numerous ways. Challenging her immediately might satisfy your personal distress with her comments, but patience will set a more productive stage for a future helping relationship.

Determining whether someone is initially coming to you in a personal, social, or academic context will be the first clue about how to proceed. Once you know something of where the person or group is coming from, then you can begin to consider other conditions affecting the timing, place, and style of your hallway relationship.

TIMING IT RIGHT

Life continues at its own pace even when someone is in a hurry. Dwan is a worrier and wants to decide what college he will attend by the end of this, his sophomore year. Ms. Navarro is demanding that change happen quickly. Gwenn will have to wait seven months before the baby is born, but in a few weeks the pregnancy will show and decisions will then need to be made quickly. Some of these problems have plenty of time for casual, short hallway approaches, whereas others require more immediacy and formal attention. Your job is to recognize the differences so that your actions can match the timing needs.

Judging the true time pressure on an individual is necessary to choose the best individual helping strategy. This may seem obvious, but when problems, people, and ideas are coming at you from all directions, panic and mistakes become commonplace. In the hallways, you need a simple triage plan similar in concept to those used in a hospital emergency room. Problems are sorted by priorities based on how quickly things need to be handled and how much survival is an issue.

Now-or-Never

Now-or-never situations leave no recourse other than to drop everything and act immediately, or the moment to act will have vanished. Examples might be breaking up a fight where one person is in danger, giving quick advice to a teacher with an angry parent waiting in the office, or consoling a child who has just found out his mother died in a car accident. Miss the opportunity to act immediately in situations like this, and you miss the chance to have a major impact.

Little to no preparation or planning is present for now-or-never situations. These instances require confidence in your professional reactions so that no time is lost. Quick consultations, definitive actions, and continual evaluation of how well your intervention is working are the keys to now-or-never situations. Recognizing when the emergency is over is also important so that you can consider other less hurried interventions.

Pressured

Pressured situations require decisions in a limited amount of time, but more than you have in now-or-never situations. These situations have significant consequences if the decisions are not made appropriately and require quick reaction or at least discussion of timely actions. Gwenn's unexpected pregnancy is a very difficult situation, and in her mind it will certainly feel like a now-or-never situation. The reality is that she has months before the baby is due, weeks to decide how to tell the general community, and at least days to prepare for telling her parents. Gwenn has time to talk, think, and plan even though she must make some decisions soon. There is often more time and less need for direct action in more situations than most people would expect.

Casual

There is plenty of time to talk, think, reflect, and plan in a casual situation, but it is important that such activities go on regularly in a more prevention format.

"My daughter Shannon was an excellent first-grade student who was panicked the first time she missed several questions on a homework assignment. She was sure that she was failing and would never catch up. To her this was a major emergency, and certainly we attended to her anxiety. But the most important actions we took were those that attended to the developmental nature of her experience. Relaxed talking about the situation in a casual atmosphere, suggesting she talk with the teacher, demonstrating our own mistakes, making sure she saw our confidence in her, and considering ways we could check to see that things were going well in the future were the supportive actions necessary to emphasize the actual casual timing situation."

This is a classic situation for developmental and prevention-focused hallway strategies that can be offered quickly and regularly to build and maintain confidence.

Long-Term

The essence of a long-term strategy is preparation for serious discussions about action, rather than taking direct action. Ms. Navarro believes the actions of people in the school need to be made immediately, and her first statements to you could be very demanding. Once her initial anxieties are settled, the problem then becomes a more realistic long-term situation. The task is to say and do things that will calm and support her while building a relationship base designed to promote more cooperative working relationships for the future. Bullying, test scores, and the way people have dealt with them in a school have a history that cannot be reversed in one short burst of brilliance. Promotion of more interdependent relationships among all concerned will be needed, and that starts with developing a trusted relationship with Ms. Navarro.

Timing is crucial in building productive relationships outside the office cocoon, but there is more to it than timing alone. Seemingly good timing must also be used in the right place to be effective.

LOCATION, LOCATION, LOCATION

> *"Many of you will identify with the first time I had to administer a standardized test. Where else could I administer a test to a large group except in the cafeteria? It was all so logical until I realized that cooks talk, laugh, and bang pans. And if the noise wasn't enough, the smell of fresh rolls and lasagna started permeating the room after the test had begun. Stomachs grumbled, heads began looking up, and students started resting their heads on the tests. Eyes blinked closed, some looked to the ceiling, and students increasingly wanted to go to the bathroom. The cafeteria was a great place for lunch, but a lousy place to give a test."*

Location is important, but what place is best keeps changing. Depending on what you need to accomplish, who you must do it with, and when it needs to happen, some places will always provide better opportunities than others. Innumerable specifics might help determine the ultimate meeting place for a given situation, but who would remember them all? Making a basic decision between private versus public and between quiet versus noisy will give you a solid start that can be adjusted as needs change.

Private Versus Public

The classes you had in graduate school directed you to meet clients with as much privacy and control as possible. Counseling was in the office and guidance lessons were in the classroom. Helping in the hallways requires another way of thinking that emphasizes the value of having others around and in less controlled situations.

Gwenn is dealing with critical life issues and is very upset about them. Her most pressing concerns call for highly private and confidential settings, but she needs additional settings as well. For example, she needs practice dealing with feelings of embarrassment over her situation. She needs support and affirmation for her efforts. Her classmates will also benefit from understanding both the concerns and excitement about the changes in her life.

After telling you about her situation, Gwenn will be looking hard to see how you react to her outside the office. Although the thoughts running through her mind in the office will be on her, seeing you in the hallways will focus attention on your reactions as a test of how others might react in the future:

Will she treat me differently now that I've told her?

Will she be angry?

Will she show caring like she always does or not, because I'm pregnant?

Will her different attention be an embarrassment or a good feeling?

Will it be OK, or will I want to run away?

The place to get these questions answered is in the mix of other people, where the real world conveys a special brand of truth and understanding.

Hallways are the places for public words and actions; things that others can see or hear. One of the worst things you can do is to try to bring your highly private office relationship into the hallways. Words and actions that show others you know something very new and different about Gwenn will do her no favors.

Hallway actions and words are best used to test ideas in the real world that have already been thought through in more private settings.

Some hallway interactions require more privacy than others.

Developing a close relationship with Ms. Navarro can produce a quiet conversation about how to best approach the staff and students with her concerns.

> *When Jean is in tears from being teased in the hallways, a quiet walk around the empty playground might be just the ticket to help her regain control before going back to class.*

Hallways are not private places, but you can achieve degrees of privacy if you use all the locations available. They can add a public dimension to your interventions that emphasize social interactions and experiential learning in multiple locations.

Quiet Versus Loud

Everybody knows why you want quiet, but why would you ever want noise in a helping relationship? The textbooks offer no answers here, but an evening at a rowdy basketball game will shed some light.

> *Dan was hooting and hollering while on the bench in a way that worried me he would go out of control as he sometimes did in school. Once he got in the game, he was a ball of energy and although he never scored, he drove the other team into mistakes with his enthusiastic play. When the game was over, he was tired, calmer, and more sociable than I'd ever seen him during the school day.*

Emotions and reactions take over in their most raw forms at these events. People who are quiet the rest of the day yell and scream things that will come out nowhere else. They are excited, involved, and their natural emotions and strengths take over from the concerns controlling them the rest of the day. For many people, it is the rigid structure in most of their ordered lives that keeps them from relaxing, growing, and learning about other exciting potentials in themselves. Noise and excitement help break down that rigidity, change body chemistry, and allow alternate aspects of a person to come into play.

Noisy places can provide relief for people in situations like Gwenn's. She can casually avoid personal conversations because of the noise, but the noise will force her to be close to people in order to be heard. The closeness in crowded and noisy hallways can be threatening, but it can also be comforting when someone needs physical closeness that is not easily asked for or given.

As a male counselor, I can walk in crowded hallways next to a female student, even brushing our arms together in a show of support with much less attention than if we were standing alone, in a classroom, or entering an office. The same is even truer for many male students who might otherwise never allow themselves to be seen physically touching another male. Noisy hallways, dances, gyms, and playgrounds are places where people are forced to be close, drop formalities, relax, and do it all with minimal stigma attached. These can be just the settings that create readiness for change.

CHARTING A HALLWAY COURSE

Information doesn't do anyone much good unless it fits into some organized picture. Ask me to remember facts and I'm generally at a loss. Factual knowledge only comes out for me when I am in the middle of a discussion, reading, or writing something that follows a simple and logical pattern of thought. Table 3.1 provides the framework of the ideas used in deciding where, when, and how to negotiate hallway relationships. Some will think through interactions they know will arise and review recent experiences to see how they did. The most organized may keep notes on people or situations, while others will only maintain a rough outline in their heads. Your task is to make use of the framework in the formal or informal ways that fit you best. The next chapter offers a set of steps to move from this evaluation of the hazards and potentials to the direct actions needed to follow through on your assessment.

Table 3.1   Hallway Evaluation Summary

Factors	Action Considerations
Willingness	
Resistant	Requires helper patience, since too quick or strong a response can turn this type off to any helping.
Responsive	A certain amount of tension and motivation creates a press for help that can be more assertive.
Overconfident	Too much confidence may require gentle reminders of the hesitancies that might slow down a decision or action.
Ability	
Able	Offer guidance and motivation for actions that fit the individual's related abilities.
Unable	Wait for direct action until appropriate abilities can be developed or until appropriate goals & actions are identified that fit abilities.
Context	
Personal	More significant personal issues generally require more privacy than hallways can provide, but hallways can later support them.
Social	Social problems can be solved only in social situations, making hallway prevention or intervention critical at some point.
Academic	When people see their problems as learning or problem solving rather than personal or social, they need to be approached from their perspective rather than what helpers might think is the real issue.

Timing	
Now-or-Never	Immediate action is required to intervene or prevent a dangerous situation with the larger problem put off until more level heads prevail.
Pressured	Something needs to happen, but a final solution is not needed immediately.
Casual	Plenty of time is available for planning for prevention, but regularity of actions is needed.
Long-Term	Preparation is emphasized by creating better conditions for more pointed discussions or actions in the future.
Location	
Private vs. Public	Offices are for privacy whereas hallway interactions will allow others to hear and see.
Quiet vs. Loud	Quiet places allow for specific verbal information communication whereas loud places demand generalities and more physical responses.

4

Courting
Captive Clients

The last job I held before becoming a school counselor was counseling in a prison. It was better preparation for being a school counselor than I ever expected. School is not the prison that some students call it, but there are many important similarities between the two environments that work in the favor of those who want to help. Prisoners and students both have required places to be during the day, specific rules to follow, and continuous direction and supervision. Learning to use the characteristics of this captive environment rather than fighting them is key to helping students outside your office.

School students spend 6 to 10 hours a day in an environment that may begin at a bus stop and end at a dance or sporting event, or with a homework assignment. They come in contact with individual and groups of peers, teachers, educational specialists, parents, and others throughout the day. Positive growth and change is directed by multiple interactions with a wide variety of youth and adults rather than by any one individual. Perhaps a teacher or counselor will make a great impression on an individual or group of students, but that will either be strengthened or diminished by everyone else who makes contact.

> *Randle was an eighth grader whose English teacher created enthusiasm in him about creative writing. He was much less enthusiastic about math and physical education where a running battle went on around whether Randle was lazy or stupid, or whether the teachers didn't respect him. His anger eventually wound up in rebellion that caused a lengthy suspension from school. While on suspension, he got involved with a crowd doing drugs, which began a physical, social, and academic down-hill slide that ended his school career and any writing ambitions.*

For every story like Randle's, there are many others in which someone made a positive difference in a student's life and others helped the difference flourish. The more people in the system who have a sense of understanding along with when and where to help, the more positive will be the climate for learning and growth. The ultimate task is then to help create the type of positive overall system promoted by the ASCA Model, even when you need to build that support one person at a time.

You know who the people that can help are and where they are. The more supportive contacts you make with traditional learners; participants in athletic, academic, and social organizations; and as members of school and public communities, the greater the difference you can make. With so many things filling your day already, the secret is to use the time you already spend in the hallways, parking lots, ball games, coffee shops, and cafeterias to your best advantage.

The general factors that go into creating quality hallway contacts are the same for everyone, but the captive nature of your audience provides unique advantages. Meeting students in locations that match their changing needs becomes possible when you know where they will be and when they will be there. Observing students will tell you when they are ready to be pushed and when pushing will be counterproductive. The more time you spend in student environments, the more you learn, and this understanding can lead to the best choices about how, when, and where to get the most from your hallway helping skills.

ENVIRONMENTS FOR CHANGE

The only legitimate reason for interventions with students is to influence the academic, personal, or social changes in their lives. Each day brings the potential to improve learning, sooth a hurt, calm tensions, or head off problems that may only be realized in the future. To be consistently effective, you need to understand three critical combinations of student environments and characteristics.

Academic Slowdown

Adults create schools for academic information gathering and skill development. This is the work of the classroom, but once out from behind classroom desks, students generally choose to deal with more personal and social issues. The result is an academic slowdown for students where formal studies become a much lower priority. Missing or ignoring the slowdown leads to misinterpretation of student actions and offering assistance where it is not wanted or needed. Recognizing student academic slowdown will improve your choices of which actions are most vital at a given time and where they are best employed.

> *Anne is a third grader whose schoolwork has fallen off drastically at about the same time her family is going through a divorce. Counseling on family issues needs to be done in the privacy of the office, but the hallways offer an additional vehicle for growth. Brief supportive academic hallway interactions can be used to extend support because the content is expected and recognized as normal public information and the caring attention and sensitivity are supportive of her whole situation.*

The counselor who had gained Anne's trust had a couple of hallway techniques she used to promote her academic efforts. She used one of them with many students who enjoyed their interactions. At times that appeared random to Anne, the counselor would pass her in the hallway, lunchroom, or at the bus stop. A "Hello Anne," would be followed by a math problem "5 times 11?" Anne would answer and give a question back "13 times 6?" that was always harder. Often the counselor didn't get the answer fast enough and sometimes she would just get it wrong. They would both have a good laugh that friends also saw as fun, and so began to play their own variations of the game.

One positive aspect of student academic slowdown is that, although academics create great pressure in class, they can often be approached with much less tension in the hallways. A teacher immediately conveys high tension levels inside the classroom when he says, "What could you do to prepare better for the next test?" The same statement made by a counselor who regularly works the more casual hallway atmosphere carries much less anxiety-provoking baggage. The difference is that academic success or failure is the essence of classroom fears, which can raise casual statements to ones of paramount importance.

Students know instinctively that their ownership of the hallways offers greater permission to accept or reject your statements. Even the simple fact that everyone is standing, anywhere they want to be in the hallways, conveys more equality and power to the students than they feel in the classroom.

The fact that students have greater freedom of choice in the hallways reduces defensiveness and increases the chances that information will be used when communicated under low-anxiety conditions.

This is the low-pressure advantage open to counselors, coaches, club advisors, teachers, and others interacting outside the normal classroom framework that can make a major difference in a student's development. Supplying reinforcements for success, quick statements to promote later thought, and emergency reminders of homework or tests can all give the academic needs of students quality visibility. They must, however, be used in proper proportion to the personal and social issues that generally make up the bulk of student priorities in the hallways.

Personal Choice

Issues that are personally seen as critical carry considerable threat for all ages, and this is particularly true as students approach adolescence. Resistance to letting adults into their personal thoughts, feelings, and worries is a common result. The opposite is true in the hallways, bathrooms, playgrounds, streets, alleys, buses, and cars where most momentous personal decisions are discussed among peers. They select the specific places and times to meet where adults are least likely to appear. These are the safe places for personal openness.

> *Those allowed to help with more personal issues of students are the people who find their way to student comfort zones and lay the groundwork there for dealing with personal issues.*

The counseling office is probably the only place that can provide the quiet, isolation, and freedom to talk openly and honestly about such intense issues, but it can be difficult to get students to the office when personal issues are being hidden from adults. Hallways and gymnasiums are not places for intense personal discussions, but they are places where you can reduce the chances of offers to help being put off.

Fighting students' personal put-offs in the hallways requires indirect techniques. This is no time to dive right in with, "I know you've got problems that we can discuss." A student hearing this quickly looks around to see who might have overheard such a stupid adult pointing out a seemingly unspeakable weakness. No matter how true the statement is, it would be denied or ignored and the student would leave the scene as quickly as possible.

A more productive approach in this situation is to be attentive, supportive, relationship focused, and only vaguely suggestive. Students are more likely to accept help with critical issues if they believe you recognize the situation, respect their limits, and will not press beyond their personal, academic, and social boundaries.

The counselor says with a smile: "Hi John. Could you take some good news?"

Or

At lunch, a teacher says, after purposely writing nearly illegibly on a student's paper, "Good work on the assignment. I'll be around at the break if you can't read my notes on it."

The time you spend with students in their own environment provides firsthand knowledge of how to best create opportunities for more meaningful discussions. Students need to be convinced that you have seen enough of their real world to interact on a more equal level and without disrupting other relationships. This strengthening of hallway relationships is accompanied by an increased understanding of students' lives that offers additional social opportunities to make a difference.

Social Framing

Social framing is the hallway tactic with the most consistent potential for having a major effect. The academic context is centered in the classroom or in quiet places where books, papers, pencils, and thinking are the essential tools. When issues take on a highly personal meaning, they benefit most directly from intimate conversations with few people.

> Because the hallways are social gathering places more than anything else, it is the social needs of students and the social framing of situations that have the greatest influence here.

Student social lives are played out in the hallways. The shy walk quickly at the sides of the hallways with their heads down. Getting to their next destination with as little interaction as possible is the goal. The socially needy go from one person to another trying to gather as many contacts as possible without missing any new possibility that might come along. These social scavengers would never get to the next class except that the hallways eventually empty out. Most students fall in between these extremes, recognizing their need for others as well as their limited ability to consistently get those needs met. One constant for all these social categories of students is that students develop clear patterns that can be recognized and used to construct appropriate social interventions.

Everyone knows a girl like Diane who moves from one class to the next in a consistent pattern: eyes on books, a rapid walk, staying out of heavy traffic, going directly from room to room, only looking up if absolutely necessary, and never attending extracurricular activities. Her words say, "Class is fine," but her hallway patterns tell you her issues are more social avoidance than academic pleasures. Once you recognize that Diane has constructed a minimal-contact social environment that eases fears at the same time it disappoints her, you can begin creating developmentally appropriate social frameworks to help.

Productive social framing should emphasize strengths and areas of confidence as new areas of weakness and doubt are gently explored. For Diane, this means the best possible construction would attach her academic knowledge and future planning to social contacts and potential relationship development. Finding Diane momentarily lingering with a group of academically oriented students would be the right framework for providing a compliment on an academic achievement. It emphasizes her strength to a group that could appreciate it. The same statement could create a social setback if made when she was near a socially focused group in which academic prowess would be seen as insignificant at best and insulting at worst. What could be considered support for Diane in one social framework would be a social liability in another.

> *Hallway social framing is best approached more as the producer of a play than as an actor or even as a director. The task is to recognize when the right people are in the right place at the right time and then make use of the situation when it presents itself.*

Unlike in the office, you cannot arrange seating, introduce issues, and ensure follow-through on ideas. Instead, you rely on others for most of the interaction and continuing contact. It is the particular people you put together, where, and under what conditions that make or break social framing interventions.

EXPANDING THE HALLWAYS

The term *hallways* has been used throughout this book as a metaphor for all those casual places outside the formal office or classroom structure. Actual school hallways are the most common places to make such interventions, because everyone visits them daily, but they are certainly not the only places. As you increase hallway interactions, you will recognize that some environments call for loud and rowdy interactions on your part while others require soothing and soft interactions for the best communication. Deciding which to use is based partly on the environment and partly on what is reasonable to accomplish.

Joining the Loud Crowd

Dealing with students at a ball game, a dance, or in the hallways often needs to be approached more like a loud concert than a school event. A parent who recently returned from a first rock concert with her child said, "My hearing may never come back, but for some reason my daughter's friends still think I'm cool. I couldn't understand the words of the songs, couldn't talk about it over the noise, and couldn't understand why people's eardrums weren't popping. Only near the end did I start enjoying myself, but I don't really know why. I was exhausted."

This parent went with her daughter expecting to listen to music, which has little to do with the attraction of a modern rock concert. She had the wrong idea, because noise, commotion, and losing oneself in the event are what young people's concerts are all about; the music is secondary. Only when exhaustion caused her to give up on her own expectations and fit into what everyone else was enjoying did she become "the coolest mom" and a functional part of the event.

The helper's role in highly charged events must often be to fit in first and worry about changing people later.

Hallways, dances, and athletic contests demand loud and public reactions in order to be accepted as someone with credibility. Students often seek out coaches, dance chaperones, and advisors precisely because they have shown their ability to enjoy and interact within these student-chosen environments. They become a part of the event by getting into the flow, speaking louder, gesturing more obviously, and clearly enjoying what the events have to offer. Some may never dance or scream, but *they are there* with a smile that shows respect for the students and their source of enthusiasm.

Changing the use of touch and closeness is also necessary to make yourself a viable participant under these circumstances. Much of the attraction of loud, public hallway events is that their very nature demands that personal inhibitions be lowered. The loudness forces closeness and physical interaction to get messages across. Aspects of relationships must be explored here that would be seriously frowned on in most situations. Boys can hug, girls can push, boys can cry, and girls can swear at these times with minimal stigma attached. Milling around at a sporting event, dancing in groups, and getting caught in the crush of a hallway are other low-risk rationales for making physical and social contacts that might otherwise be deemed unacceptable. When you become comfortable interacting in these situations, you open new dimensions of potential issues to be discussed and strategies to be used.

> *A teacher described her experience when she became a soccer referee for a girl's league. "These girls on the playing field were so different from what I saw in the classroom. Here they were strong and determined to win, and when the game was over, they wanted to talk with me about how they did. It was so different from class where they had nothing to say to me and couldn't wait to leave. But after officiating for just a couple of games, they did acknowledge me entering and leaving the classroom, were more attentive in class, and sometimes even approached me outside of class. It was neat and a totally unexpected benefit."*

Learning the locations where individuals and groups make themselves visible in loud ways, and becoming recognized as fitting in, greatly increases adult credibility. Enjoying the interactions without giving up your personal and professional beliefs makes you a particularly strong role model and change agent. Effective modeling in these places requires establishing a harmony between the loudness and brashness of the situation and the calmness and soothing qualities developed in traditional professional training.

Creating Calm

Joining in the turmoil of a hallway location does not require giving up your beliefs to be effective. Many times it is the symphonic blending of behaviors as you stick to your most cherished beliefs that makes for the most effective helping.

The "cool concert mom" was relieved to see that the drugs that appeared all around were not a part of her daughter's experience. She was thankful she didn't have to draw that line but knew that she would have, if necessary, to stand up for her most firmly held principles, never mind the law. She had enough hallway understanding to recognize that the kids already knew where she stood, and she would not need to set down the rules beforehand. Simply being involved and modeling demonstrated and supported her beliefs, and the trust she showed in the young people fostered better relationships. It was a blending of more obvious "cool mom" involvement, less obvious "holding back" nonactions, loud enjoyment, and quiet confidence that created a solid opportunity for adding a new positive dimension to the relationships.

There are specific actions you can use to create a limited amount of quiet and privacy in even the rowdiest situations. Consider the following actions to gain small pieces of semi-privacy in raucous environments:

Obvious physical movements that are different from the norm of the environment get people's attention (e.g., try subtle first and go to more obvious as needed).

Making yourself larger gets people's attention (e.g., shoulders up, sit straighter, stand taller, or, more subtly, raise your eyebrows).

Shrinking yourself can hold attention and bring a person closer to you where communication is more effective (e.g., lower shoulders, hunch over, or lean down).

Lowering your voice level increases attention once you have it.

Trying to change a commonly loud, public environment into a private, quiet one just doesn't work and makes you look out of touch to boot. Effective hallway counseling with students comes about by first fitting into the rhythm of the environment so that your messages will be taken as more credible. This increased hallway credibility strengthens your influence with students as they become ready to make use of your help.

REFLEXES AND PATIENCE

Knowing where students are most of the day tells you much about the time pressure they are under and how much need there is for you to help. For example, classroom time can produce pressure for students but little demand for you to act quickly, so patience becomes a key timing factor. Once students explode into the hallways, however, it is your reflex reactions that will be tested. Keeping in mind a few classic situations allows you to make the best use of the skills you have already developed.

Hustling Reflexes

Emergency and pressured hallway situations come at the most hectic times and are often accompanied by extreme emotions. Explosions immediately after classes are commonplace as students collide physically and emotionally.

Jean was in tears near the end of a tense lunch period where major confrontations arose as everyone was trying to get in their last, best verbal shots. The heat and pressure of an afterschool talent competition increased the chances that any statement made would be taken as a personal insult demanding aggressive words or actions.

The counselor realized that hustling behaviors were the keys to successful hallway helping. Waiting for one of the girls to come to the office with a problem was out of the question. Thinking about future plans would be a mistake. She recognized that hustling to make actions that were focused, immediate, and directed at de-escalating tensions was essential.

The counselor acted quickly but casually by walking toward the girls' table while still giving attention to those at other tables she passed, making comments and smiling with them. She didn't stop at the girls' table, but kept her slow pace, and as the girls recognized her, they stopped and the counselor said, "Good luck at the talent competition this afternoon. I hope you can take some deep breaths and enjoy it." She paused long enough to see that their emotions had settled a little, and then continued on to the next table.

During these pressured times, you need to remind yourself of things that you learned long ago but can be forgotten in the rush of the moment. The most basic reminder is to always use the lowest possible intensity of confrontational action that will ease the situation. High-intensity actions raise the stakes for everyone and should be used only when the stakes are already dangerously high. As a colleague once put it for me, "You don't play an ace when a nine will do." The reduced threat produced by low-intensity actions allows for more flexibility in future actions. Only when low-intensity actions prove ineffective in a given situation should you begin using higher levels of intensity. Don't forget those directions I was given long ago, to start low and not use your best cards unless they are clearly needed. Table 4.1 provides a list of low- and high-intensity actions.

Table 4.1   Low- and High-Intensity Actions

Low-Intensity Actions	High-Intensity Actions
Ignore	Punishment
Brief eye contact	Glaring eye contact
Subtle nonverbal movements	Pointing
Friendly humor	Angry reactions
Touching	Grabbing

The counselor recognized the need to act quickly in order to short-circuit the situation before it became worse. Her approach to the girls was casual enough that the girls didn't feel like they were being singled out for behaviors they knew were problems. She also never directly approached the girls' frustration, anger, or even Jean's tears. Instead, she offered a low-intensity level of intervention that calmed behaviors and allowed for some recognition of what was raising tensions. She knew that if this didn't work, she would be in good position to increase the intensity of her actions as needed.

When one effort doesn't stop a hallway confrontation, spur-of-the-moment alternative actions are essential. There is no time to go back to the office to search for new techniques or consult with supervisors. This is the time for your most ingrained skills to take over if you will let them. Increase safety factors, acquire more support, and look for every possible opportunity to lower tensions and stop the escalation.

Hanging Out

Students often think they need emergency help when, for the most part, their problems call for a more casual approach. The organization of the school day, classroom seating, and regulated periods all create a system designed to reduce emergencies. These nonemergency times call for hanging out in the hallways, where your specific goals and direct actions underlie a casual veneer.

Unlike with the hustling needed during actual emergencies, you can actually give some forethought to a hanging-out approach.

Mary is a freshman whose mother has gone into the hospital. Deciding to make a couple of short, physical, supportive contacts with Mary during the day can be as easy as offering smiles, caring looks, or brief encouraging touches on the arm. They provide Mary strength and support without stirring up all her emotions as a direct conversation might do.

Your planned contact with Mary takes only seconds and allows for numerous other hanging-out contacts before and after. A couple of minutes in the hallway is all it takes to congratulate Jim for an improved test score, to ask Jocelyn whether she has taken her new medication, to point the new student in the right direction, to ask David to look out for the new student, and to show interest in the football victory with an upraised fist for Albert. Planning hanging-out efforts to provide timely support, direction, rewards, casual admonitions, and reminders to as many people as possible simply makes what you probably do naturally more consistent and effective.

Patient Presence

Emergencies and planned interactions are important opportunities, but many others are available to you. Most chances to influence others during the day relate to more long-term objectives. Relationship building and future-oriented student objectives are those that require short, simple, subtle—and most important—consistent contacts over time. They call for maintaining a patient presence in students' lives.

Professionals who are seen dealing exclusively with personal traumas, testing tragedies, and scheduling screw-ups will be seen as the "shrink" or "administrator" for people with "big" problems—the kind of person you want when you are in trouble but not the person you go to for "little" worries, "normal" anxieties, or "just" thinking about the future.

> *Students want adults for everyday support and guidance who show genuine understanding of their lives, appreciate them, enjoy their lives as an outsider, and are easily accessible.*

Taking time to maintain a patient presence in students' lives on a regular basis is really quite easy and can be done in numerous places during regular daily travels: being visible between periods, walking through afterschool practices, sitting in different places in the cafeteria, attending a dance, or mingling at a ball game. Major planning and brilliant words of wisdom are unnecessary. Consistent physical and emotional attending are the keys to developing confidence and building relationships over time.

The timing of hallway interventions will vary depending on the balance between emergency pressures and the ability to focus on long-term goals. Selecting the appropriate balance can sometimes be identified simply by observing emotional levels. One of the factors that affects those timing needs and emotional levels is the academic, personal, or social nature of the issues involved.

REACTING TO READINESS

I will never be faced with as wide a variety of readiness levels as in my first school counseling position where I handled all grade levels. Kindergartners were willing to try just about anything I asked, but their level of thinking, talking, and sitting didn't fit my training at all. The seniors, on the other hand, had plenty of ability but were unwilling to work on anything that didn't fit very precise needs and situations. It took a series of disappointing counseling efforts to teach me that the variety of school student readiness characteristics was going to be much greater than what I had faced with adults. I would need to pay close attention to what someone would be willing and able to act on effectively.

Student readiness varies with age, gender, culture, and daily events. What I discovered was that this inconsistency can work in your favor as well as make things more difficult. Fluctuations in student readiness make it possible that any minute of any day may be just the right time for a student to use and accept helpful actions. The trick is to recognize high-level readiness instances and act based on the abilities and willingness presented.

Behavioral Buttressing

The skills and knowledge that make up ability are what are taught most directly and most often in schools. Hallways, lunchrooms, playgrounds, gyms, and streets are the worst places to introduce knowledge and abilities, but these are great places to clarify and fortify learning in real-life situations. Behavioral buttressing of the abilities taught elsewhere is the best use of hallway helping to improve the ability aspect of readiness.

Gwenn had no idea how to start explaining her pregnancy to others when she first came to see her counselor. In the privacy of the office, the counselor gave her a book and then discussed with her the specific information and actions she needed to consider. The counselor reminded her of health class lectures and handouts even as she scoffed at the idea that these could have any practical value. The hallways would have been the absolute worst place to supply such information or to have Gwenn study and process it. On the other hand, they are exactly the right place for Gwenn to practice what she learned.

A teacher came to the counselor to let her know that Gwenn was pregnant. She had overheard Gwenn telling a couple of close friends. This was the kind of follow-through the counselor hoped Gwenn would do so that she wouldn't have to carry the burden alone. To strengthen the behavior and show support, she found a way to casually approach Gwenn and her friends when they were talking together, and seemed in a positive mood. Her first words were all that were needed: "Hi ladies."

The girls couldn't wait to talk with the counselor: "We've been planning how to tell Gwenn's mom and then to get the word out to others. Want to hear what we were thinking?"

It was in the hallways where Gwenn started the process of letting others know. That is where the counselor's information and encouragement began to take hold. Expressing her fears and needs, and wondering how to respond to looks and comments of others started with her closest friends. Now it was not Gwenn alone, and the girls knew an adult was there to help them who would have solid opinions, but also respect their choices around what to do next and when.

Practice in the hallways provides the opportunity to evaluate skill development and set up reinforcements for productive new behaviors along with disincentives for behaviors that don't work.

Leave the responsibility of introducing concepts, skills, and abilities to the classroom teacher, the office session, the tutor, and the parent. Sticking to the functional strengths of hallways to buttress the learning of abilities will increase your hallway helping potential and decrease the chances of making serious mistakes. Limiting what you try to accomplish will also leave more time to attend to a student's willingness, which is taught less directly or effectively in schools.

Wary Willingness

Teaching students what, why, and how to act is a far cry from getting them to take appropriate action. Many of us forget this from time to time as we try to teach students life skills they already know, but simply choose not to practice. The reason for their lack of action is generally not some missing piece of ability, but instead a lack of willingness to match the risks of potential action.

> *Hallway helpers watch for student willingness to risk in different situations, respect willingness levels, and improve the support systems that can appropriately increase the willingness to act.*

Student willingness has to do with matching changing comfort and confidence levels with risk levels that escalate or de-escalate as situations evolve. Interventions that match student discomfort and lowered confidence with high-risk situations are bound to fail. Reading willingness levels wrong can lead to pushing a student into a situation in which embarrassment will be the primary outcome. Reading willingness correctly can put a student in a situation where he or she can find success in overcoming a meaningful obstacle.

When high anxiety best defines someone's willingness level, offering support through reinforcements or encouraging safe actions are the only viable techniques. It is not the time for direct confrontation or logical reasoning, as one counselor reflected to me.

"I think of a boy whom I have followed for a couple of years with casual support. It seemed like almost overnight he changed from a normal boy with reasonable concerns and problems to suddenly becoming a

member of a local gang. I struggled with how to approach him, knowing that any attention I gave when around this gang would turn him away from me. It had to be casual meetings and a slow process in which I gained the understanding needed before any direct help could be given.

I found a reason to see him where he worked and another time we chatted briefly when I saw him at the fairgrounds. A comment here and there in the school hallways were other brief moments. It took a long time for him to let me know more about what he was going through, but it was better than approaching him directly, only to be rejected for an even longer period of time."

There are also those times when rejection of your efforts or anxiety over consequences is not what is driving a student's willingness to act. These are the times when students are confident that they can speak or act effectively in a given situation. Your role in the case of confident students encompasses several basic hallway tasks.

Let them act as they will. Encourage confident students to act on their own beliefs and ideas. The only times to reconsider this are when you are specifically invited to offer direction or when you are afraid the natural consequences of a student's actions are both serious and irreparable.

Point out potential actions sparingly. Nothing squashes a student's confidence like overdirecting them. Successfully carrying out your good ideas will provide nowhere near the potential growth as actions they choose by themselves.

Arrange for appropriate reinforcements to be in place. Students need to be reinforced most for their positive personal and social actions. Spend your time putting mechanisms in place to reward productive hallway behaviors. These might include bringing together people who will naturally be appreciative of positive actions, getting yourself

(Continued)

(Continued)

in the right place to be able to compliment a positive action, and creating a schoolwide reward system that supports positive actions in the hallways. Every high school has an athletic trophy case, so why not create another for "Hallway Heroes" that calls attention to the social and personal accomplishments of students and graduates.

Help evaluate the natural consequences. Confident students will act on their own no matter what you say. Your efforts should attend to the aftermath of actions and helping people evaluate the consequences of their words and behaviors.

Be ready to pick up the pieces. One of the dangers of confidence is that ability can be misjudged based on poor comparisons to past successes. Your analysis of what people are trying to do and their ability to do it puts you in a position to catch those who have had a failure. Remember also that failure is a learning tool, and it is not your role to prevent failure.

You can serve students by getting them back on their feet when they have been knocked down and helping them learn from mistakes. The seemingly unlimited and constantly changing characteristics of individual students make work with them exciting, rewarding, complex, and sometimes nearly impossible. Using hallway techniques is a way to expand the opportunities for seeing and interacting with students in their most natural environment. The more comfortable you become with that environment outside your office, the more consistencies you will see in their world. This more accurate picture of student needs and behavior patterns will create opportunities for more consistent and effective developmental use of multiple, brief hallway encounters with students.

The increased opportunities to help students that hallway encounters provide can be multiplied even further by including adults in the hallway helping model. This is no easy task, because not all other adults will have your abilities and motivation. The next chapter offers ideas on how to use hallway strategies to help encourage adults to become more effective at developing their own hallway potential.

Table 4.2   Captive Client Keys Summary

Captive Client Keys	Need to Recognize	Action Guide
Environments for Change		
Academic Slowdown	Time out of class is not time for formal academic lessons.	Support academics indirectly, without pressure and integrated to personal interactions.
Personal Choice	There is less need to accept what you say or follow through on directions in the hallways.	Give maximum emphasis to allowing for choice in type and content of interactions.
Social Framing	Others will have abilities to teach and help that you don't.	Arrange situations where significant others can provide appropriate influence.
Expanding Hallways		
Joining the Loud Crowd	There are loud places were kids are more comfortable than adults.	Meet and find pleasure in environments that fit others but are not your style.
Creating Calm	There are places where settling behaviors need emphasis.	Voice, motion, and words to calm in nonthreatening ways.

(Continued)

Table 4.2 (Continued)

Captive Client Keys	Need to Recognize	Action Guide
Reflexes and Patience		
Hustling Reflexes	There are intervention or prevention emergency situations.	React immediately with level of intensity to fit the situation.
Hanging Out	Consistent support is needed but at a low level that fits into everyday situations.	Take planned, casual, simple actions to support in a relaxed atmosphere.
Patient Presence	Large problems take time for solutions to appear and take hold	Use actions to support small steps in the right direction for progress rather than solution.
Reacting to Readiness		
Behavioral Buttressing	Formal learning needs hallway environment support.	Create opportunities to reinforce formal lessons.
Wary Willingness	People are not equally ready for adult connections in all circumstances.	Choose times and places to interact where people will be most receptive.

5

Activating Adult Motivators

Making a realistic commitment to provide the best possible service to young people carries the obligation to involve others who are part of the school environment. This task of getting adults on my side seemed like a straightforward task as a newly indoctrinated professional. Books and instructors explained how the roles of counselors, teachers, administrators, mental health professionals, parents, secretaries, service employees, and community members were all designed to form an efficient working team. A few days on the job made it clear that such a "team" is not easily created, strengthened, or maintained—no matter what the books say.

Getting the most effective teamwork from professional and nonprofessional adults requires more personal persuasion than rules, regulations, or theory. It requires personal time and attention to the human being inside the formal role. Even the best of us can forget or ignore the personal needs and limitations of adults.

We sometimes act with adults in ways we would consider uncaring, unprofessional, or even unethical if we did the same with students.

Years ago a wonderful counselor from Oregon taught me this important lesson at a national convention. We met at a crowded reception and quickly found a common bond in our work to improve school climate and frustrations over not making all the progress we sought. Vicki was using joy, enthusiasm, and stories she found in music to improve the environment of whole schools. I have no musical talent at all, but I loved what she was doing and we eagerly searched for ideas on how to improve on her successes.

Vicki's only major frustration was that she couldn't reach the level of involvement and enthusiasm from professionals and other adults that students willingly gave her. We knew that greater adult commitment was critical if the enthusiasm and actions her programs generated were to continue after she left. So we whined together for a few minutes about how responsible professionals and parents are "supposed to act." Tears welling up in Vicki's eyes made it clear she had recognized something else that was missing:

> "I'm just realizing that I don't treat adults in the school with the same care, attention, and forgiveness that I treat the students. I attend to students as real people with human needs and fallibilities while treating professionals and parents more like robots that are required to do their jobs as expected. Why should they be personally excited like the students? Why should they trust in my ideas and me? Why should they think this would be good for them as well as students? I don't follow through on my most important beliefs with adults the same way I do with students. That's what's wrong!"

One side effect of Vicki's tears was a simple confirmation of my status as anything but the life of a party. More important, however, was the realization that we needed to be more attentive to the human side of adults in order to tap their maximum potential for helping children. We recalled how our most effective professional relationships were those in which personal understanding, trust, caring, and support were obviously present. The less significant a role these played in the relationship, the narrower was the scope of our ability to help. Vicki and I left the party excited that we had a new direction for being more effective in schools: We vowed to be more attentive to the human being inside the adult.

It's easy to become overwhelmed with the seemingly unlimited complications surrounding the personal, professional, societal, and situational characteristics of relationships. The more we learn, the more complex they become. We know gender, age, race, culture, developmental stage, family functioning, economics, intelligence, creativity, and a myriad of other factors significantly affect relationships. It's enough to make you want to throw up your hands and say, "I quit! I can't handle any more!"

No professional can take every personal and situational characteristic into account all the time. We just don't have that much mental and emotional capacity. Successful professionals categorize knowledge in their minds so they can quickly identify a few motivators that will most likely get desired results with a given person or situation.

> *Three general motivators of adults in school situations that need continual care and attention from the effective hallway helper are power, vulnerability, and joy.*

You can feel confident that no matter what other issues are involved; these general motivators will play a major part in getting the most productive school involvement out of any adult.

POWER

Power is a word that becomes overly formalized in schools, where it is clearly attached to positions, ranks, and titles. We tend to presume that those who hold formal titles and positions have power and the will to use it, whereas others without rank lack power altogether. As schools become increasingly based on structured tasks and roles, a greater emphasis has been given to this formal power and less on personal relationships. Such a situation might have some validity if formal power actually worked as well as planned, but it never does.

The informal power of a persistent student, loud parent, willing teacher, reliable bus driver, or trusted counselor is often much more influential than that of any formal position. Unfortunately, the fearful teacher, defensive administrator, embarrassed parent, or hesitant counselor will too often give up potential personal power and influence because of their misconceptions or anxieties. You can vastly increase your hallway influence by being regularly attentive to three aspects of power:

---

1. The commonly exaggerated and often inappropriate attention given to formal positions of power

2. The massive amount of informal power that goes unrecognized

3. The effects of people's power misperceptions

Creating and adapting to change in ways that are embraced by the largest number of people is best supported by strengthening the informal power available to all individuals and groups. Hallway relationship building recognizes formal powers that serve to maintain stability within the school, but it is informal power that hallways influence best. One person with formal power can "tell someone to act," but it is the much greater numbers of people with informal power available to them that will determine if, when, where, and how appropriate actions will be.

The more people you move from the position of uninvolved bystanders to people who recognize and act on their informal power potential, the healthier a community becomes through greater sharing of power and responsibility.

The effective use of informal hallway power incorporates a variety of "soft" strategies. These soft approaches downplay demanding forms of power that often lead to resentment and defeat in hallway interactions. Your formal power interventions are best saved for critical times in private sessions where egos will not be so challenged. Following are some samples of an almost infinite number of soft hallway strategies with adults:

Build cooperative approaches rather than individual initiatives.

Maintain a relaxed, confident posture in tense, difficult situations.

Listen and reflect much more than telling and directing, encouraging mild hallway confrontations on issues, but avoiding hallway confrontations on personalities.

Use mediation for win-win situations rather than conflict for who-wins.

Demonstrate respect even when you don't feel it's deserved.

Never comment on private information in public.

Encourage only actions that can be accomplished in public.

De-escalate tensions rather than giving in to frustrations.

Schools that achieve the most positive changes in academics, discipline, and climate invariably report how all groups of adults and students feel more involved, encouraged, and empowered. It is an empowerment that authority cannot delegate, but instead must be identified and implemented through personal insights and supportive relationships. These are the supportive relationships and soft-power strategies you can use in normal daily interactions to promote adult strengths and help adults overcome misconceptions and self-doubt that stand in the way of their best possible efforts.

VULNERABILITY

The degree to which people feel vulnerable to harm will influence how much risk they take and how much effort they give in a particular situation. Encouraging people rather than demanding change requires attention to the origins of an individual's tension and anxieties. One essential step to hallway success is recognizing the different causes of adult feelings of vulnerability related to schools. Only with these understandings in hand can hallway strategies be selected with the confidence they will lower or sometimes raise an adult's levels of vulnerability to make them as effective as possible.

Our actions toward others frequently ignore how vulnerable many adults actually feel in school situations.

> *Students may get report cards, but it is adults who are under the most pressure when the question of what went wrong comes up.*

Adults are the ones who receive the eventual blame and feel the guilt for a lack of student learning, violence, inadequate school conditions, a lack of resources, or a poor home environment. Just thinking about the potential failure of the youth in our care is enough to tie knots in our stomachs.

Adults handle vulnerability in a multitude of more and less effective ways, including concern, talking, organization, determination, tears, anger, blaming, screaming, and silence. They may strike out, politely ask for attention, isolate themselves, or switch reactions at times and places that seem to make no sense at all. Although some reactions are more socially acceptable ways of demonstrating "vulnerability" than others, they all represent a common concern for the survival of an adult's professional and personal self-worth.

Hallway effectiveness increases as you give more attention to those things that make an adult feel vulnerable, recognize what conditions trigger the reactions, and act to mediate the vulnerability. Someone's vulnerability is rarely brought up in conversation. More often, it is attended to by adapting interactions to take the threats into account. Only when an adult's vulnerabilities are held in proper perspective can people make the most of their abilities and find the excitement and pleasure that exist all around in school interactions.

JOY

The joy of personal involvement in the lives of young people and other adults is a major force motivating positive work by adults in schools. If consideration of individual power and vulnerability seem like minefields to traverse, joy is an area that you can approach from a more straightforward direction. Adults want good things for children in schools, and they will be most happy and useful when you help them find active, creative, effective, and personally satisfying ways to be involved.

A simple smile is recognized by aware adults as the unspoken message, "Thank you so very much." They understand when a parent's sigh of relief means, "Bless you for helping." And they are the adults who take pleasure in the little ways that appreciation is shown for their efforts. Those who work the best and the hardest for schools are the ones who realize the joy in their efforts, and the more people can be helped to recognize that joy, the better for everyone.

Using techniques that tap an adult's sense of joy at being involved with children and the school greatly increases your overall influence on the total school environment as well as on those specific individuals and their children. Joy-tapping asks for little more than calling attention to pleasures and successes already present, but perhaps not readily recognized.

It is easy to overlook the everyday personal joy of doing good while being fully involved with people. Adults in particular are presumed to "know" that they are in the middle of enjoyable and worthy circumstances, but that is a false presumption.

We all need continual reminders to examine and cherish our personal sources of joy and accomplishments.

Hallway helping takes every opportunity to encourage positive, reflective looks. The external rewards for joy-recognizing actions are an invigorated atmosphere and more motivated adults seeking ways of being productively involved in the school.

The influence that comes with official positions is an important component of maintaining social stability and physical safety. But the nature of official roles and formal responsibilities, as well as the physical structure of buildings, offices, and classrooms, can also cause a system to underutilize individual motivation, knowledge, skills, creativity, and outside input. Brief, casual, personally empowering, threat-lowering, and joy-illuminating hallway strategies serve to strengthen the system by reinvigorating adults who come in contact with it.

These three school-related motivators apply to all adults, but not in equal amounts nor in the same ways to everyone. Teachers, administrators, staff, parents, and others are influenced differently based on their unique situations. These differences must be taken into account in order to increase the respect and influence all adults feel, thereby creating a better balance with formal power gained from the system.

TAILORING STRATEGIES FOR TEACHERS

Teachers have far more contact with students than anyone else during the school day, giving them enormous potential for influence. Tapping that influence potential requires strategies that encourage teachers to take a more accurate, positive, growth-oriented, and enjoyable approach to their workday. Specific techniques are selected based on an understanding of the power and vulnerability of teachers and taking appropriate actions to reflect them.

Balance Power and Vulnerability

A major influence on teachers' motivation is the extreme contrast in their power and vulnerability depending on whether they are inside or outside the classroom. Inside the classroom they have virtually total official power over where students sit, what they do, when they talk, and what they discuss.

> *Outside the classroom unofficial influence reigns as students pay more attention to those people they value and respect as persons and less to those in formal positions of power.*

This influence transition makes teachers much more vulnerable outside the classroom than inside. Many never become comfortable with the continuous shifting of necessary perspectives and skills. In order to protect themselves and bring consistency to their lives, they often settle for either ruling the classroom with an iron fist or being a buddy in the hallways. Using either direction as a model creates a situation in which you experience an influence vacuum, greater vulnerability, and less enjoyment in one of the locations than in the other.

Your hallway skills and knowledge can help teachers become more comfortable at shifting their approach to students and parents from "classroom boss" to "respected individual" and back again as the situation calls for it. This hallway assistance can be offered and reinforced within real-life situations rather than in counseling or training sessions. For example, you can

Make sure to support the teacher as an equal or better in every situation, thereby confirming his or her power and reducing feelings of vulnerability.

Give recognition to the different situations, feelings, and behaviors involved when conflicts occur between classroom and hallway pressures.

Call attention to the different ways some adults gain influence in one setting and give it away in others. Ask reflective questions on why that might be so and how one could change for the better.

Note the differences in who students pay attention to outside the classroom and explore what could be done to gain such influence.

Showcase Success

Teachers know what makes them feel good at school; they just don't take time to pay attention to it. They can easily miss the look of excitement and satisfaction in a student's face that resulted from their efforts. When they do give that look the attention it deserves, their sense of success and appreciation becomes a highlight of the day. Those looks are there to be seen when a student does well on a test, makes the volleyball team, finds a new friend, wins an award, or finally understands an idea that has continually escaped her. Unfortunately, teachers get tired and frustrated, and are often too busy, too tied up in thoughts, or too burned out to see these signs of their own success.

> *Teachers often miss the best rewards for being teachers: the parts that go furthest toward making them caring, motivated, and student oriented.*

A particularly pleasant hallway strategy is highlighting the joy of teacher successes when they may be going unrecognized. The task only takes looking for the positive outcomes that teachers cause and pointing them out to the teacher, as the following examples show.

"John is awfully proud. You must be pleased with the progress you helped him make."

"Your choosing Vera to introduce that new student around was perfect for her. Did you see how proud she was to be in that position?"

"I bet Warren's mother never expected such a friendly welcome. She really left pleased, didn't she?"

"Can I sit in on one of your classes sometime? I hear kids talking about working their butts off there and liking it. I'd love to see it."

"The principal seems relaxed; you must have coordinated that parent/ student tutoring project to run more smoothly than she expected."

These samples are more than the simple positive reinforcement they might appear to be at first glance. You are not really giving reinforcement at all but instead calling attention to reinforcements that are naturally present. The better you come to know the school, teachers, and students, the more obvious the reinforcements become. Using them to help teachers see the everyday joy they create provides the positive outlook that will be good for everyone.

Multiply Low-Impact Contacts

There are plenty of opportunities to work with teachers in casual settings before, during, and after school, so there is no need to get everything done at once. Using conservative small steps is the hallway helping rule as you work for progress over time through multiple low-impact contacts. Leave the time-limited, difficult decisions to private places where concentration is easier and more time can be taken to make quality plans.

Professional issues have a particularly good fit with the multiple low-impact contacts model. Everyone has unspoken expectations that teachers will be professionals virtually all the time and certainly when they are in a school setting. Reacting to teachers in this professional context conveys permission to talk about important issues without drawing the undue attention that an overheard personal or social discussion might attract. You can use this professional context to indirectly approach any number of other issues. Consider just one personal and one social context example to start your thinking:

Personal—A teacher depressed over marital problems will not be cured but could still benefit from being given positive support for a student's success or recognizing his students' excitement about class.

Social—An inappropriately self-isolated teacher could be socially encouraged by your seeking information through a casual discussion of a school issue that included several teachers.

The low impact of these interactions has long-range value because of the numerous opportunities available, and it is essential because of situation and time pressures. Teachers in the hallways have a lot going on around them. They must simultaneously evaluate what just happened in class or elsewhere; act on what is happening right now; and prepare for what they will have to do shortly. They cannot deal effectively with major issues in the hallways without ignoring more immediate concerns. Numerous low-impact interactions fit these timing needs best when they focus attention on what is happening, what just happened, or what is about to happen. The closer your interactions are to the immediate time press of the teacher, the greater impact they are likely to have.

As the importance of issues rises, you must increasingly seek more private places and additional quiet time. The office certainly fits these criteria, but it may also provide more formality than would be best. Middle-ground places that fall between hectic hallway environments and formal offices are places like the cafeteria when it is not lunchtime, the local coffee shop, the teacher's lounge, the local library, or just taking a short walk during a planning period, before school, or at day's end. This small sample of middle-ground locations offers a positive reason to be there, more privacy than the hallways, a slower pace, and the opportunity to take a break from the immediate teacher responsibilities. Your selection of the right amount of formality, casualness, privacy, and necessary time is based on your evaluation of the teacher's need and readiness to be helped.

Hear the Unsaid "No"

Teachers have students, parents, administrators, and state regulators who are continually pushing them to do more with less. That they become self-protective and hesitant about accepting anything new or different should be no surprise. In a way, it is amazing that teachers continue to seek improvement on professional, personal, and social fronts as often as they do. You can support this growth motivation with strategies that attend to the struggles that influence teachers' willingness and ability to think new thoughts, experience new feelings, and try new behaviors.

Most teachers experienced a relaxed pleasure in the school environment when they were successful students, but once they became teachers that environment took a more threatening turn. The successful student learned how to enjoy taking in information and giving it back as required by an authority figure. The switch to being the authoritative information source and controller of the process is not an easy one. This new role contains greater pressure to meet more people's expectations than any student experiences they may have had. How willing a teacher is to recognize and act on your hallway interactions will be directly related to how well you attend to his signs of unwillingness.

It would be nice if professionals who were unwilling to do something would just tell you "No," but it usually isn't that simple. Pride and determination to meet other peoples' expectations often push us to look for indirect ways to avoid something rather than to take the direct approach. Consider some common signs we have all recognized when helpful initiatives are greeted with an unsaid "No":

Looking elsewhere while feigning attention to you (I can't give you my full attention and therefore cannot be held to my answer.)

Suddenly nervous movements of head, eyes, feet, or hands (This contact is making me anxious, and I might lie to get away.)

A quick acknowledgment of your contact followed by immediately exiting the situation (I had to leave too quickly to be responsible for what my answer would be.)

Looking around for someone else as if really needing to see that person (I can't attend to you because there is a more important need.)

Avoiding eye contact as you approach (I cannot run away, so I'll pretend I don't see you.)

"Sure, just talk to me again about it" (No way will I consider that, but I'll get you off my back, and maybe you'll forget.)

It is important to tread carefully regarding the willingness of teachers, because they have so much invested in looking professional and not making mistakes.

Too much pressure often results in teachers actively avoiding your input and even subverting your work with others.

Always leave room to lower the intensity of relationships based on your recognition of discomfort and unwillingness on the part of a teacher.

Principal Investment

The individual most often responsible for setting the overall tone of a school is the building principal, so influencing that person's efforts can have major significance. Holding the highest formal position brings the principal maximum credit for a school's successes and also the most blame for its failures. This combination of formal power and high vulnerability is a potent mixture that drives principals in one of two directions. Those who focus on gaining credit and success become highly visible and aggressively push for productive changes. Others seeking security from their vulnerability shy away from the dangers of visibility and stifle change. Leaving the principal out of your intentional hallway interactions discounts a major influence on school climate. On the other hand, giving direct attention to casual interactions with administrators can go far toward invigorating a school's atmosphere.

Hallway efforts to influence principals focus on perceptions of a principal's power rather than official job duties.

When staff, students, parents, and principals themselves have faith in the position and the person, tremendous power becomes available for positive use. You can help create a healthier school climate by spending some energy caring for this fragile power and feeding ideas and information that bring out a principal's best for those you care for most.

Reach Out First, Often, and Productively

If you want schools to move in directions you desire and principals to make decisions you think are best, then take the initiative rather than "hoping" for things to go your way. Regularly make the first move to get your agenda on the table and keep it there in personally productive ways.

A friend of mine (Jack) was a teacher who regularly got only a portion of this effort right. He was in the principal's office all the time and always had an agenda for what needed to be done. The part he never got right was to offer those ideas in productive ways. He actually treated the principal much as he did students in class, but the messages were more suited to the teacher/student/classroom model than to dealing with a principal:

- Here's what's wrong.
- This is what needs to be done.
- It's up to you to fix it.

It should be no surprise that he never got what he wanted from the principal. All he really did was turn the principal off to his ideas. The principal was a good person, but when the teacher came back again and again with only his agenda, what was wrong, and the idea that it was always the principal's responsibility to fix things, the principal gave up listening. He would pass me during the day and say; "Jack was in" with a smile and a small side-to-side head shake. I would simply match his smile to recognize his frustration.

Jack's behavior toward the principal did have one positive effect. The principal knew there would be no considering alternative views with Jack, but he did have that kind of relationship with me. So we would talk, often over coffee and away from school where I made a point of being periodically so that we would meet regularly. These were productive discussions that generally helped confirm some of the principal's ideas, added credence to new ideas that he did not initially accept, and reinforced my opportunity to influence school decisions.

The key is to build a personally meaningful relationship where trust, understanding, and credibility are essential parts. This is not something that happens with a twice-per-year meeting. It takes many short and comfortable interactions to break down the defenses based on the differences in levels of power and responsibility.

Feed Organizational Needs

The way to a principal's heart is through improving the orderly flow of ideas and actions. Give confirmation when things are working right; publicly support productive changes; help clarify the realities of problem situations; and offer alternative procedures for problem areas. Many of you will question whether your principal will listen to any of this—and you may be right to wonder. But although they may not give you credit for it, the fact remains that administrators get most of their ideas from others whom they trust—and one of those others might as well be you.

Widespread acceptance of the ASCA Model has been a real boost to this aspect of dealing with administrators. The focus on the whole school, verifiable progress for all students, and assessment fits right into the organizational demands felt by principals. It provides a structure that matches the principal's goals for the school and multiple reasons to discuss school-wide and districtwide issues.

The social and emotional issues that have historically been closely associated with counselors, psychologists, and social workers have now been formally given their rightful place in relation to individual achievement and the school climate that affects everyone's progress. The ASCA Model has defined our roles as holistically involved in student growth and achievement, which is a perfect match for what administration needs to make happen. We have the opportunity to be their working ally in the improvement and maintenance of an overall effective school system. Our task is to recognize it and talk in those terms with administrators.

Personalize Relationships

The most effective principals have personalized relationships with a wide variety of students, parents, community leaders, and teachers. Occasionally reminding them of names, people to commend, upcoming community events, or the special times in a student's, teacher's, or parent's life encourages more personalized contact with more students and adults. The more of these contacts they have, the more likely they are to respond to the human needs of the school.

One counselor with an excellent relationship with her principal would take a yearly calendar and write in birthdays and other key dates in the school for the principal and give it to him each fall. The principal would then send small thoughtful cards on birthdays and other special days to staff. It was a simple and pleasant relationship that, over time, went a long way toward strengthening the counselor-principal relationship and added to the sense of personalization throughout the school with the sense that the principal cared for them as people. This counselor could have sent the cards herself, but she realized that, in this case, improved relationships between the principal and staff were more important than those between her and the staff, which were already positive. It was a choice for the school rather than for her personal reward.

Maintain Touch With the Real World

It is remarkably easy for principals to become isolated in their offices. One principal put it this way: "Problems, headaches, and more problems; all this without taking a step out of the office. I'm a damn captive, and when the problems are gone, I'm afraid to step outside and see what's coming next."

Effective principals are visibly active in the hallways, classrooms, playgrounds, and community. The more of that you can promote, the better it is for the school. Inviting a principal into a classroom guidance session, dragging one out of the office to enjoy the hallways, or generally calling attention to these times and places where they can see what the rest of the real world is doing are all pluses for increased understanding and realistic decision making.

APPRECIATING SPECIALISTS

Teacher and principal positions are given a much wider range of official powers than the remainder of the staff. Counselors, psychologists, social workers, secretaries, custodians, cooks, and bus drivers have much less authority to direct student thoughts and actions. The result is that staff must make many more questionable judgment calls on how to best fulfill their roles. What value is placed on their ideas or actions? How should they raise difficult issues? Whose toes will be stepped on? How much effort should they make in situations that don't directly affect their responsibilities? When do they get involved, and when should they keep their noses out of a bad scene? This vagueness about the breadth of specialists' roles in promoting the overall school climate is the key factor to consider when approaching hallway interactions with them.

Although most schools have specialists who do their limited jobs well, the best schools have staff that are involved in school affairs well beyond the confines of formal job descriptions. The custodian who attends school board meetings, the psychologist who keeps score at basketball games, the secretary who attends faculty meetings, and the bus driver who is an assistant football coach each add to a more unified school community. These actions break down role barriers and encourage a more holistic approach to maintaining a healthy school. It is just these types of actions that hallway strategies can encourage and support by validating contributions, reinforcing professional responsibilities, and promoting expanded involvement efforts.

Validate Specialties

Respect is the foundation for any positive relationship, and it can be first communicated to school specialists through validations of their position, work, and related accomplishments. People in these positions do not get the automatic recognition when a school succeeds that comes to teachers and principals. Unless they are provided specific reinforcements to validate themselves, problematic feelings of disinterest, discouragement, and resentment are likely to become the norm.

Hallway strategies with staff begin with communicating casual and consistent appreciative recognition of the value and quality of each specialist's work.

Promoting staff member efforts that go beyond specific work assignments can be accomplished only when cooks, secretaries, psychologists, and counselors feel valued for the work they are specifically hired to do.

Attend to the Little Extras

Hallway strategies that influence the most people give attention to those ideas and actions that go only "slightly beyond" basic professional obligations. This form of social-behavioral shaping fits the nature of specialists' positions that do not encourage them to step outside specifically assigned tasks. Cooks cannot be required to advise students, counselors wouldn't be told to help keep the buses running, and secretaries aren't asked to teach English skills. Reinforcing broader school involvement on the part of competent but uninvolved staff members requires regular attention to the smallest of steps. The bus driver who comments on a student needs to be thanked immediately and reminded of the value of the comment at a later time. The cook who one day adds a few hand-picked flowers to the lunch counter needs to be specifically complimented. The psychologist who leaves a handwritten note with an assessment needs encouragement for taking the extra time to personalize. Remembering to recognize and support staff members who do the little extras is no new technique, but it is an easy one to forget in the rush of the day.

Support Public Risking

The further staff members go beyond specified responsibilities, the greater are the risks they take. Public support is needed to encourage such actions, because even the most innocent movements away from designated roles make well-meaning people anxious and feeling threatened. Someone will question the audacity of the secretary who first volunteers to teach staff and students what she learned at a recent workshop. A custodian and social worker who come together to a monthly board of education meeting will be bombarded with mildly stated and harsher unstated questions about their possible motivation for such an unheard of act. When the assistant coach of the volleyball team is also a cook, many will wonder, what is the story here?

> *Publicly, physically, verbally, and socially showing appreciation for people who step into uncharted waters is central to hallway helping of staff. These are the ways you demonstrate the belief that individual human beings have greater value to the school community than any job description can ever specify.*

Hallway strategies emphasize the value of people's specific roles, attend to personal factors, and promote risk-taking actions that make greater use of their talents. This expansion of school staff involvement also increases the ability to tap parent and community resources.

FORGING PARENTAL PARTNERSHIPS

A frail mother with three small children standing just ahead of me at the supermarket handed the cashier some food stamps for groceries and just enough cash to pay for one small book.

The little book promised easy steps to making better students out of the hellions running around her. I doubted if anything could make a difference, but I also wondered what treat or even necessity this woman was passing up for the hope of providing a better education for her children? What other things did she forgo to improve their learning? One quick look at bookstore shelves demonstrates that this woman may have been poorer than most but similarly motivated. The enormous number of books on parenting and parental relationships with schools is convincing evidence that the amount of information and adult resources available outside the school walls is tremendous. What is needed is a forging of cooperative partnerships that invite and invest this wealth of adult resources into our efforts with young people.

The most successful schools are those that have formed solid relationships with parents and communities. The mutual involvement of these groups builds understanding, trust, and commitment to each other by breaking down the barriers of brick walls, formal power structures, and social snobbery. Hallway helping techniques are partnership-building tools that reach beyond formal offices, structured classrooms, and official positions to meet people on common ground and more equal footing. They are the casual means by which parent-school tensions can be reduced and the natural joys of learning recognized.

Power and vulnerability are the most important sources of tension when outsiders come into contact with school personnel.

Parents are likely to sense that they will be looked down on because of the school personnel's training and formal roles with students. Whether or not professionals feel or communicate these ideas, the perceived power differential raises the stakes for outsiders and makes them highly vulnerable. Any interactions with the goal of forging more equal partnerships must decrease this perceived power differential in order to realize the positive benefits.

The joy of seeing children learn and knowing you play a part is the strongest positive motivator for adult involvement in education. This is a common bonding element for school-community partnerships that hallway strategies can regularly bring into everyone's consciousness. Hallway helping points up the pleasures of helping children learn in multiple ways, whether it's preparing them for a test, reading together, arguing over new ideas, or finding the best bargain at the supermarket. These are not complex strategies; they require little academic study; and they don't take great concentration. What they do demand to maintain their value is frequent use with as many adults as possible.

Locate Relaxed Adults

Relaxed occasions and locations are the times and places to make yourself a real person in the eyes of nonschool adults. These places are little league games, street corners, church bazaars, blacktop basketball courts, carnivals, and fishing holes.

> *Find out where the adults you want to affect go to relax,
> take yourself there, and bump into them not so accidentally.*

Watch, relax, be involved, and get a sense of what your potential partners are like in their comfort zone. The strongest partnerships are the ones that share relaxed time as well as business time.

Meet Where Adults Are Confident

Equalize power differentials between yourself and outsiders by meeting where they are most confident. Meeting parents in the office, classroom, or somewhere else in the school is great for professionals, but these are also places where a parent's confidence is lowest. When a parent is asked to meet at school, chances are 90% that something is wrong and they will arrive prepared for the worst. Parents' homes, offices, a mall, or a coffee shop can be used as casual alternative meeting places to reduce tension, increase parent confidence, and promote the sharing of responsibilities.

Find Something to Support

Building relationships with a wide variety of adults requires supporting the most obnoxious adults as well as the most pleasant. This is no easy task, but it is an important one.

Long-term outcomes are best when you highlight something valuable about the individual in every relationship interaction.

I once had a parent come up to me in a parking lot, furious about his daughter seeing me for counseling. I was intolerant of the fact that he abused his daughter and wife, angry at his accusatory and threatening behavior toward me, and I resented his ruining my weekend. I didn't hide my feelings, but it took all the parking lot patience I could muster to also express my appreciation for his coming directly to me and then to explain how, when, and where he could file charges against me. I figured I'd give him the rope to hang himself by encouraging him to bring things out into the open. As I expected, no charges were filed, but surprisingly, he later asked me to help him find a counselor. He told me that no one had ever tried to help him when he was that angry, and when he calmed down, he realized I was someone who could be trusted.

Give a Psychological Massage

Let business issues, answers, and problems occasionally go by the wayside when someone needs special stroking. It is easier to justify this in casual relationship building than in the office or classroom, where work, goals, and time on task generally take priority. Give everyone a break once in a while and just make a couple of people feel better about themselves.

The effort can pay partnership dividends later as people realize something of your caring for them even when you wind up on different sides of an issue.

Regardless of the results on the issue, the sense of caring promotes continuation of the partnership and potential for progress.

Repeat Yourself

Anything that can be done once in the hallways is better done repeatedly. One brief supportive gesture, friendly word, statement of praise, or expression of comfort may have little value in itself. Repetition and consistency make the long-term difference.

Human nature dims the joy of one interaction quickly and causes doubt about its real meaning. This is particularly true for adults who have years of negative learning experiences that must be unlearned. Only when you consistently meet, greet, and attend to people with positive casual interactions do you cement understanding of the major benefits of a solid partnership.

Make Preemptive Contacts

Private interactions often deal with problems that have arisen, whereas hallway strategies emphasize relationship building before a crisis. It only takes a little experience to recognize what crises are likely to occur, when to expect them, and which parents will probably be involved. This information should help you head off negative crises, soften the impact of others, and even promote crises that have positive potential. Hallway strategies are much more effective when they are used over time in developmental ways.

Meet Outside More Than Inside

This is a simple numbers issue. Making briefer hallway contacts with parents off the school grounds than within the building lowers tension levels, improves trust, creates a more equal responsibility for partnerships, and produces stronger relationships over time. Once you recognize that you are having regular contacts with a parent in school, it should signify that your roles are likely becoming rigid and one-sided and call for spending more time in the parent's world. Positive telephone calls and individual notes count for these contacts, as well as shopping mall hellos, ball games, and home visits.

Get Down

This is a basic concept that is very easy to forget. To downplay your potential threat and increase the confidence of a parent, always sit, stand, or kneel lower than them. Take the smaller chair, stand on the next lower step, lean on something to shrink your height, or kneel if you must, but don't ever stand when a parent is sitting. This is essential body language and goes a long way in convincing someone that ideas and actions are more important to you than official positions.

Building more equal parent partnerships requires you to make the extra gestures of openness, respect, and equality in order to show that your part in the relationship comes more from who you are than what position you hold or what extra education you have. They will increase your influence on the entire school community and, in turn, bring you some of the personal and professional benefits we all desire.

6

Steps to Hallway HELPING

> **H** asten Normalization
>
> **E** valuate Context
>
> **L** ocate Common Goals
>
> **P** ragmatic Action Selection
>
> **I** nitiate Multiple Connections
>
> **N** ormal Adaptations
>
> **G** ive Space

For all the work I do with counselors, teachers, parents, and administrators, it is student interactions outside the classroom that provide me with the greatest dose of humility. I love the work and get plenty of reinforcement, but still, the second-guessing starts for me on the drive home. "Did I have enough control of the situation or maybe I should have done something more?" "What took me so long to act?" "How could I forget something I'd done hundreds of times?" "What in the world caused me to say that?" "Did that parent think I ignored her?" I may have had years of successful interactions with students, staff, and parents, but I still have those all-too-human symptoms of forgetting, missing a cue, stuttering, or taking actions that I'd like to change later. Reviewing the brief HELPING steps in this chapter as reminders of things I already know helps me keep on track, even if they don't cure all my human weaknesses.

Understanding people in the hallways has little value until you turn that knowledge into action. A solid plan for taking quick, appropriate action, evaluating the results, and deciding what to do next can provide the direction and confidence needed to do the best job possible. The brevity and frequency of hallway interventions requires a plan that lets you immediately tap into the skills and knowledge your training and experiences have already provided.

The demand for reflexive action in the hallways is similar to increasing pressures being felt throughout the business and counseling fields. These pressures have brought *The One-Minute Manager* (Blanchard & Johnson, 1982) to business, whereas *Single Session Therapy* (Talmon, 1990) and *Brief Counseling That Works* (Sklare, 2004) have influenced the counseling profession. Each model offers similar general guidelines: Gain control of the situation, relate immediately, set limited goals, support strengths, move quickly to action, continuously reassess, and finish what you can before you lose your client. These are guidelines that work, and the following steps will help you adapt these brief intervention concepts to hallway settings. The starting place in each case is to bring as much stability as possible to the situation so your knowledge and skills will have the opportunity to make a difference.

STEP 1: HASTEN NORMALIZATION

The essence of hallway interactions is that they take place within normal life experiences. It is a model of fitting into life's rhythms as people naturally interact with it. Most of these situations will present themselves in reasonably safe and secure atmospheres. The exceptions need additional effort. In either case, every relationship requires some level of safety and security to ensure that learning takes place. Whether it is the office, classroom, or the much less predictable hallways and gymnasiums, some sense of stability is essential.

> *The first goal is to normalize the situation by gaining just enough control so that those who would help have the opportunity to do so and those in need can recognize and accept the help being offered.*

Emotional Safety

Influencing a school administrator like Ms. Navarro is a situation that is not physically dangerous, but does have emotional safety issues. Most school principals regularly deal with all kinds of conflicts that arise in the school and they are never at their most approachable when in the middle of such a conflict or following it. Intervening to change this person's way of thinking and acting toward staff and students will not be taken well when it comes at a time of high stress.

Times of high stress for Ms. Navarro or anyone else call for giving a person time and space to bring him- or herself back to normal. If you have developed a trusting relationship and recognize the ways the person deals with stress, you may also be able to provide some support when the person is ready for it. A viable starting place for hallway helping is to hasten the person's sense of being in a normal situation where your influence can appear as a natural occurrence rather than as therapeutic or teaching.

Physical Safety

Creating physical safety can require more direct, immediate, and sometimes more forceful actions to achieve normality than emotional safety. Emotional harm can have devastating effects, but those effects do not take place as quickly as physical harm. The higher the level of physical danger, the faster normalization reactions need to take place. People generally recognize this need, but they often take inappropriate actions that can worsen the problem rather than de-escalating it.

When Dan is punching out another student, it is time to put good counseling skills on hold for a while. The first action is to de-escalate the situation and bring official rules and personnel into action. Listening, reasoning, and understanding will be effective shortly, but not until safety and security are reestablished.

Subtlety can be just the right model where situations suggest little danger and are relatively normal. But as situations become more out of control, subtlety approaches worthlessness. These are the times to make use of the system with its defined roles and rules to gain and maintain a semblance of order. The following guidelines help make the best use of all the resources available to you. They are not complex, but they are easy to forget.

Guidelines for De-Escalating a Situation

Gaining control is essential. Doing this by force and demanding behaviors are usually harmful for long-range benefits, but sometimes essential if enough danger is present. Shoot for long-range benefits by using less force and fewer demands as danger levels decrease.

Follow official rules to help gain control. Discounting rules is legally problematic and justifies rule-ignoring behaviors on the part of others. Work on changing poor rules formally after the emergency has passed.

Carry out individual responsibilities is the message to be conveyed to everyone. Usurping the rightful role of the student, principal, teacher, parent, police officer, and so forth because you think you can do it better robs those individuals of power. They are then likely to either abdicate their roles altogether or fight you.

Communicate accurate tension levels. People need to have a realistic sense of the tension they and others are feeling in order to react appropriately.

You may need to calm some people, whereas others will need their anxiety levels raised to match the realities of the situation.

Everyone's individual or group concerns will be given specific time later. This needs to be understood clearly by all. Logic, reason, and understanding are at their low points during high-stress situations. Right now, the only need is to "get the situation and people's reactions under control."

Delay future decisions. Poor decisions are made when emotions are high and events are out of control. It is better to delay decisions than to make poor ones under stress that you regret and need to change later.

These guidelines serve a dual purpose by helping you settle yourself. Highly stressful situations will ratchet up your own adrenalin along with the physical and emotional levels of others. The need is to act quickly, but as calmly and logically as possible, which the guidelines should help you achieve.

Gaining control of the situation will help others and you set the stage for using more traditional helping skills. Logical reasoning never wins out in the middle of a screaming argument. Only after the situational bleeding is stopped can you begin preparing relationships for growth and renewal.

STEP 2: EVALUATE CONTEXT

Identifying individual needs and the contexts in which you ought to work with them are essential. This is where the context of the person's problem (private, social, or academic) is taken into consideration. The degree of stability acquired during the first step provides the space to begin considering the concerns of those involved. Professional training most directly prepared you for this step that emphasizes observing, listening, thinking, and focusing on those in need.

Choosing Personal, Academic, or Social Context

Dwan wants you to take the responsibility of finding him the right college and ensuring that he will be admitted. This step is the one in which you decide whether your actions will be guided by following his stated directions, "find me a school," or by attending to his avoidance of immediate responsibilities and directly facing self-confidence issues. The "finding a school" issue sounds like an academic context, whereas the responsibility and self-confidence issues are more personal and social. Which of these contexts you will give attention to first is the decision to be made.

You will need to know more about Dwan to see what he really needs. What has he already done? How much pressure is he really under? What role do his friends, parents, and teachers play in his decision? Dwan's situation is not likely to be as immediate as the panic he demonstrates, so it is important that you don't get caught up in his need to rush. Perhaps the most important question for a hallways decision is, "What can he talk about first and with ease?" If he has little relationship with you, then a discussion around what he's looking for in a college (academic) might be easiest to start. If you have had previous personal discussions with him, then a more personal topic, like why the panic right now (personal) or where are your friends in the process (social), might be easiest to begin a conversation.

The Context no One Else Wants to See

An individual who is much more likely to have her needs ignored to the detriment of herself and those around her is the principal, Ms. Navarro. You may be as frustrated by her insensitive approach to people as any other staff member, but it is at this point that you need to recognize her as a person with her own set of personal, social, and academic problems that could benefit from your attention. A decision to disregard the context of her needs, as others who are frustrated will do, would be easy in comparison with Gwenn's pregnancy or even Dwan's anxieties. You see the fear and anxiety of young people who are hurting, and the reaction is to understand and help. For Ms. Navarro, the first reaction will likely be to her professional status rather than the personal needs that could be driving her beliefs and actions. Many people will use her professional position as an excuse to ignore her needs: "I deserve better than the way she treats me; like my ideas don't count. She's the principal and she ought to know better, or the superintendent ought to set her strait. We'll see how her plan works when no one listens."

This common attitude has its seeds in frustration and evolves most often into undermining actions. Whether the actions are the undermining type or direct confrontation, they confirm for Ms. Navarro that others don't care about her needs, which only serves to reinforce her position that people won't listen to her unless she demands it. The demands, of course, only make the situation worse.

> *The hallway helper's task is to see the personal context of the problem and seek ways to break the cycle that can only serve to hurt the climate and success of the school.*

The task of working through Ms. Navarro's personal frustrations and individual needs is one most of us would actively avoid if given the choice. It can be difficult, personally taxing when we have lots of other things to do, and we may even agree that, "she should be more professional about this and relate more appropriately!" Whatever you personally feel, this is still a key person who directly affects the students and adults around her on a daily basis. The road to helping the school and all those involved make progress goes at least partially through Ms. Navarro. Avoiding her professional and personal needs makes everyone's work more difficult, stressful, and less successful. Attending to her needs in conjunction with the goals of others can improve the relationships and success of everyone in the school and provide the opportunity to focus on the common goals of the school and those within it.

STEP 3: LOCATE COMMON GOALS

Helping in the hallways seeks to blend the goals of two or more people into one concerted effort. A seventh-grade girl may want to spend more time with friends to feel more accepted, whereas a supportive teacher might see her need to spend more time on homework and study that will better secure her future. These two could develop a conflict-ridden relationship if they continue to focus on their disparate goals. If, however, they can be helped to reach agreement on a common goal, such as developing joint student projects or group study techniques, they will have the basis for a helpful and productive relationship.

Finding common goals among people in the hallways and identifying brief interactions to encourage them lets you spread out your effectiveness and use more of the available positive resources. The more you know about the strengths, weaknesses, hopes, and dreams of the people around you, the better you will be able to establish and make use of such common goals. The secret is to keep those goals modest and achievable. Encouraging people to spend their lives working for world peace may be laudable, but helping them say something peaceful to a person they don't like is a much more achievable first step. Setting modest goals, achieved in a small step-by-small step fashion, is the model for finding hallway success.

As you learn more about Dwan, you find that he wants to get accepted to a college and be away from everyone here as soon as possible. He has been frustrated with his father, who believes Dwan is a loner and really needs to gain a better understanding of himself and the world by interacting with more students. They butt heads consistently, with both feeling the other isn't giving the needed attention to their ideas and needs.

One aspect of becoming helpful in the hallways is to find ways to help match one person's or group's goals with another's who sees things differently. Energies applied in the same direction are more likely to make a difference than those applied to divergent goals. Competing goals also result in antagonism and frustration, which can cause both sides to eliminate what could be an important long-range goal.

> *Two can get to a goal by going in the same direction more efficiently than having a tug of war to determine in which direction they go.*

In an ideal world, there would be ample opportunity to bring Dwan and his father together for a series of conversations that could lead to better understanding. Unfortunately, the needs of schools generally don't provide such opportunities, and this is where hallway opportunities can prove valuable. Here we seek ways that might encourage Dwan, and perhaps his father also if the opportunity presented itself, to experiment with the other's point of view.

We might help Dwan begin to see his father's goal more clearly if we could connect him with other students who have complementary college goals. For example, it is reasonable to expect that Dwan is a friend of Ted, who thinks in similar ways, and that both are weak at developing peer relationships. If you can get Ted working on the goal of developing better peer relationships, then your potential to influence Dwan increases dramatically. The closer the three of you can get to common, formal or unstated goals that are modest in nature, the more progress is likely for Dwan, Ted, and others they might touch.

You might also find the opportunity to briefly connect with Dwan's father at an extracurricular or community event. This is where you could drop a key hint or two about how to deal with Dwan without passing judgments about one side or the other.

> *"Dwan is a solid person that I've come to appreciate at school. He needs to have people express confidence in him and his efforts, but when they do, he reacts very positively. I imagine you've noticed that at home with you as well. If he can find that kind of trust from others, I know he will make some sound life decisions."*

Gwenn, too, would benefit from developing common goals related to her pregnancy with her parents, her teachers, and even her friends, making these relationships more supportive. These are not the fake commonalities often expressed as, "Whatever you want, we'll be here for you" and "We're behind you all the way." Well meaning as these may be, they don't reflect the necessary joint goals of a quality relationship that normally require negotiating different individual needs.

Publicly confirming common goals worked out elsewhere is a perfect role for hallway relationships. For example, as Gwenn's friends become involved in her advancing pregnancy, you might recognize efforts to improve their eating habits for the baby: "It looks like you are all eating a little healthier nowadays." The identification and strengthening of common goals is essential if you are to go on to more direct actions with confidence that they will work for you.

Step 4: Pragmatic Action Selection

The most effective ways you have found to help others in the past will come into play at this stage. One counselor told me that after a series of hallway interactions she counted at least five theories she had partially used. She saw a rational emotive flavor at times, took behavioral actions to reduce inappropriate behaviors, and the Adlerian in her kept trying to understand the whole picture. Most of you will start by being attentive and then choose different directions guided by what has worked best in the past. Theory that served you well before will also have value in hallway interactions. Just keep in mind that the practical value of your actions will be determined by which verbal, physical, and social strategies are most appropriate.

Verbal Strategies

Verbal strategies are given the most attention in counselor and teacher training. What to say, when to say it, and how to say it are critical issues in any orientation. How you choose your words for counseling or teaching will not change so much in your hallway helping, but the ways in which you use them must change.

The calm, quiet, encouraging voice used effectively in the office will be lost in the hallways, at a dance, or at the basketball game. There are no verbal alternatives in these situations: You either get louder and more aggressive or you give up on verbal skills.

Dictating a quiet atmosphere in the hallways is not possible, so you must adjust to the level and tempo of a given environment.

The pragmatic verbal changes you make require more flexibility rather than learning anything specifically new. Switching from speaking softly in close, tense situations to being loud in crowded, noisy situations is a major change, because everyone has clear preferences in this area. It is no small task learning to express all you want effectively in a few chopped words in a crowd rather than using the elaborately clear explanations you can provide in an office. And emotions such as excitement, joy, frustration, and sadness need to be exaggerated in crowds well beyond the subtle differences we can communicate in private. This required verbal flexibility also demands that you make matching physical changes to be effective.

Physical Strategies

The *physical* strategies you choose for hallways demand greater variety and practice than those that work in the office. Communicating different levels of trust, attention, and objectivity, and so forth in the office is all done from basically the same sitting position with minimal movement. Adjusting to the complex movements required in the hallways is no easy matter. Even the simple act of conversing while walking down the hall demands a great deal of coordination.

Mobile hallway conversations can be quite laughable when you think of all that must actually be accomplished at once. Walk at just the right speed so as not to step on someone in front or get run over from the back; match your stride to your conversational partner; watch where you are going; maintain eye contact; recognize, consider, and decide how to use other people who might be listening; have a goal for the conversation; and last but not least, speak intelligibly. A few choreography lessons might be in order for even the most graceful among us.

Closeness and touch are the most sensitive physical differences between hallway helping and office counseling or classroom teaching. The formality of the office or classroom provides consistent rules for physical closeness that are not available in less formal situations. Adjustments come in many forms, as the following samples demonstrate:

Physical Hallway Strategies

- Giving physical signals is more important in hallways because of all the turmoil.

- Simply being present can convey tremendous caring.

- Your smile may be the only one someone recognizes all day.

- A brief squeeze of the shoulder may be the only available way to effectively communicate, "I care, and you're not alone."

- A little harder squeeze might also say, "Don't do what you are thinking," and get it said in the privacy of silence.

- A simple high five can communicate how well things went, are going, or confidence in how they will go.

- Be creative and develop your personalized physical signals to communicate your positive approach.

Ethical guidelines don't relate clearly to the area of touching and distance outside the office because the rules are so vague. Greater exaggeration and wider variation of behaviors required for hallway conditions do not lend themselves to clean, safe, and specific rules. Whether hallway behaviors are ethical or not will most often be judged on the basis of loosely constructed social mores rather than regulations. This makes it critical that you understand the social guidelines in your community, their degree of flexibility, and how to use these social factors to your advantage.

Social Strategies

Social strategies are the human arrangements you make to facilitate interactions of others. These are situations created to bring people together or keep them apart in order to promote productive social interactions. Only the most naive social do-gooder would see angry people in the hallway and suggest they "get together after school and make friends." Effective social action in this case encourages angry individuals and groups to temporarily remain separated in order to reduce tension levels. Appropriately changing social conditions can reduce tension and buy time for future progress under healthier circumstances.

Dwan's situation is not a dangerous one, but it would benefit from more social contact. You might ask him to meet you in places where your interactions can lead to other relationships. Those places are in the hallways, the cafeteria, and the local hangout where people you want him to meet congregate regularly. You might find, as another example, that Ms. Navarro loves cats. Finding a way to encourage a discussion around cats with some key students, faculty, or staff would help create an environment in which barriers to interaction could be reduced and understanding gained on a personal level. In both examples you are using social strategies to build relationships. In each case, you are trying to arrange social situations that will bring the right people together under optimal conditions for the greatest overall good.

Pragmatic Opportunities

Verbal	Physical	Social
Low level during quiet	Physical signs = silent words	Arrange meetings on their turf.
Louder as noise level rises	Presence shows caring	Connect via commonalities.
Silence for thinking	Smiles for support	Play together.
Calming tones and words	Unobtrusive touch supports	Find what someone loves.
Support as part of the message	High or low five for success	Food brings people together
Nothing allows other reactions	Creating your personal signals	Kindness promotes caring.

STEP 5: INITIATE MULTIPLE CONNECTIONS

A key advantage that hallways have over your office is the availability of many more sources of information, feedback, action, and reinforcements. Using these multiple resources to help only one person at a time, as you might well do in the office, is a poor use of hallway potential. The dynamic mix of people and the vibrant nature of hallway life work best when a maximum number of people and needs are met at once. Continually seeking ways to have meet multiple needs by the interactions you facilitate is always a preferred hallway strategy.

> *Dwan needs more social interactions and some reality checks on school and college, as well as the information he wants regarding picking a college. Matching him with Ted, who has similar as well as different needs, was a step in the right direction. Finding ways to encourage their communication with juniors and seniors would*

increase social and reality connections for both boys as well as help them gain information. Working with Dwan and Ted in the context of other students will also boost your knowledge of other students who could also use similar ego bolstering, additional relationships, non-pressured practice at helping others, and social skill development.

Making hallway connections between Dwan, Ted, and older students is best done by small, subtle interventions. Being in the hallways on a regular basis gives you multiple opportunities for creating casual interactions that would go unnoticed if you were not out there every day. Consider, for example, that between first and second periods Dwan and Ted are on the other side of the school from two juniors you want them to meet, but just before lunch they are in rooms next door to each other.

The clear choice for a subtle intervention would be the natural meeting place and time just prior to lunch. You might purposely meet with the juniors at that time for some casual conversation and take advantage of that interaction by calling Dwan and Ted over when they appear: "Hey come over here a minute. . . . You know these guys (the juniors) have been picking colleges for months, and you could learn from them. Hey, I've got to run. Let me know how it goes."

This situation promotes connections between people who all have the chance to meet their personal needs at the same time they help meet the needs of others. Emphasizing mutual benefits and multiple opportunities increases the likelihood that any intervention will succeed. Taking the formal, "let's all get together in my office" out of the equation encourages a more natural environment for peer relationships to develop. Finally, you can physically leave the situation to the students, which would be out of place in the office but absolutely expected in hallway interventions. You leave the boys with ideas, connections, encouragement, and methods to explore each other's ideas within the realities of their hallway lives.

I don't live in a fairytale land any more than you do, so we know that any single interaction like this is as likely to go nowhere as to have a major effect. That's one reason why many professionals stop trying or quit in frustration. What they forget is that the more interactions you effectively promote, the greater the expectations, the possibilities, and the potential. Even in the worst-case scenario you gain.

Multiple connections made in the world outside the classroom can be as obvious as seeing people get numerous needs met immediately or as subtle as realizing that one, virtually unnoticed step toward a more productive relationship has been taken. Recognizing these results can be as good for you as for others. Recognizing the small steps forward and bits of success guard against personal burnout and promote work satisfaction.

> *The more people whose lives you are consciously dealing with, the more successes you are likely to see and the better you will feel about how you use your time.*

Changing people and their environment is the long-range goal, and you will get frustrated if you try to gain major results too quickly. Change based on subtle influences, overcoming resistance, undermining entrenched negativism, and molding an environment rather than one individual will not get done in a day. Patience, flexibility, and trust that good things develop in small steps are traits you will have to emphasize lean on in times of frustration.

STEP 6: NORMAL ADAPTATIONS

There are only two things that create a need for adapting your actions: failure and success. Failure on your part to do the right thing, failure on the student's part to progress, failure of the system to work, or various combinations are threats that should push you to continually evaluate outcomes and redesign efforts.

Your chosen profession is helping people, and failing at that strikes at the heart of your personal and professional being. Recognizing failures and weaknesses provides the impetus to reconsider actions and search for better alternatives. Not recognizing failures or ignoring them dooms you to similar failures over and over again. The result is that every training program warns of things going wrong, shows you how to recognize them, and teaches how to make corrections.

Failure may be a recognized reason for making adaptations based on results, but many fewer people see how success also requires adaptations. Any intervention that produces positive results produces change along with it, and when change occurs, reassessment and redesign of efforts are necessary to match the new circumstances. The greater the success, the more we need to redesign and alter efforts.

> It is just as incumbent on us to evaluate and adapt after successful efforts as it is to change our strategies based on failed attempts.

When Progress is Positive

Consider these reassessment and redesign needs in the context of possible interventions with Gwenn, who now wants to tell you all about her successful conversations with her mother about her pregnancy. Her mother was distraught but eventually understanding, and together they began planning for the future. The success in one situation changes the goals Gwenn must now face. Long-term goals such as planning for the birth and school after the baby is born become increasingly timely. Other short-term goals such as informing the father-to-be, her friends, and then the whole school will need more immediate, but only temporary action. The changing goals require new skills, revised relationships, and the ability to deal with constantly changing demands. Your task is to continually revise hallway strategies and not get locked into those that worked in the first successful situation.

When Tactics Don't Work

It is also possible that Gwenn's interactions with her mother could have gone poorly or that she could have hidden away until more problems arose. I have learned from working with teenage pregnancies that, although the general fears and needs may be similar, my interactions and techniques need to be very different with each situation. What worked for one young woman seemed to be of no value with another, and I never knew just what would work until the first attempt was made. Only after trying one reasonable tactic, watching how things worked or didn't work, and then adjusting my next effort to fit the results did I finally make real progress.

Assessment Resources

Productive reassessment and redesign of hallway efforts requires the use of the resources available from multiple sources. Some information will come from words as people describe how they met or didn't meet goals, were hurt, or were supported. Other information will come from visual clues of posture, facial expressions, and other physical reactions. Still more comes from your own reactions as frustration, excitement, disappointment, or elation are clues about what you may be experiencing emotionally but not cognitively. Only by using all these sources together can you realize the best of your helping abilities.

The interactive nature of hallway relationships requires that solid evaluations and adaptations look to the total environment for information. Watching how others respond when one child abuses another tells you about available levels of fear, concern for human suffering, coping strategies, and ability to unite for a common cause. How a child's relationship with his mother is changing offers clues about what you can expect from her. How her friends treat Gwenn when she is around versus how they discuss her when she is not tells much more than Gwenn's words and emotions alone. Each piece of information adds to your understanding of how strategies are working and offers directions on how to revise your actions as the situation demands.

STEP 7: GIVE SPACE

Successful relationships can become addictive for experienced professionals and students alike. It feels good to help and to be helped; to love and to be loved; to appreciate and to be appreciated; to support and to be supported; and to be successful with someone or some group. All these good feelings make it hard to let go when the student's need becomes independence from you, as it eventually must. It is even harder when students want to hold on and your job becomes one of forcefully pushing them into less secure relationships.

One benefit of hallway relationships is that they produce less obvious individual contact and influence than traditional counseling relationships, which makes letting go easier. You are never quite sure what brought about good results. How does anyone know for sure whether the critical support and influence Jean needed to overcome her victim status came from you or the people and situations you helped facilitate? Did you temporarily lower tension levels that calmed Dan's temper down, or would it have happened by itself? Did Gwenn's interactions with her mother go well because of your influence or because of Gwenn's and her mother's own abilities and motivations? Did Dwan's new relationships really come from you or were they bound to happen all along? The better you become as a hallway helper, the more you will spread around the apparent responsibility for change and encourage positive independence. The most effective hallway helpers might even wind up asking themselves, "Did anyone even recognize what damn good work I did?"

The student who clings to you may make you feel important, but that should not be confused with success. The overattached student is uncomfortable with other normal student relationships, and your ethical responsibilities direct you to increase those other relationships and decrease your own. The overattached professional is usually one who has seen real progress, gets confirmation from the student, and enjoys the interactions, and thus comes to prefer more contact rather than working harder to decrease contact. The ethical concern of putting the student's needs before your own becomes the key issue. Both cases point up the need to develop natural sources of support within the hallway environment and continually push others to use those sources.

Hallway helping is not a random set of actions. Effectiveness over time is achieved by employing a consistent pattern of decision making, action, evaluation, and adaptation. This basic action model can then be used to deal with a variety of students and adults in numerous situations.

Step	Objective	Sample Actions
1. **Hasten** Normalization	Provide safety, reason, and opportunity for positive change.	• Six steps to gain control • See to both emotional & physical safety. • Use subtlety when little danger is present. • Use the system and other people as danger becomes greater.
2. Evaluate Context	Know individual's or group's perceptions and situation at a given time so help comes in their perspective, not yours.	• Listen • Observe • Empathize • Keep your ideas out of the conversation.

Step	Objective	Sample Actions
3. Locate Common Goals	Have two or more people working on the same goal to promote unity of thought and effort.	• Begin individually to reduce potential for false agreement. • Judge the distance between goals. • Begin with the smallest common goal that could actually be achieved.
4. Pragmatic Action Selection	Select actions that fit the uniqueness of the people and situation.	• Verbal strategies emphasize information and loudness level. • Physical strategies emphasize expressions, position, and touch. • Social strategies bring people into comfortable contact.
5. Initiate Multiple Connections	Expanded personal connections increase feedback & support needed for continuing growth.	• Connect people with those in similar situations. • Use people with different situations to expand experiences and learning.

(Continued)

(Continued)

Step	Objective	Sample Actions
6. **Normal Adaptations**	Use follow-up actions based on evaluation of past actions and situational changes.	• Observe changes in people and the situation. • Listen to comments. • Reconsider information and decisions from steps 1–5. • Choose new actions based on evaluation.
7. **Give Space**	Reduced or eliminated role in the helping model.	• Reduce your role as the individual creates other sources of support. • Reduce your role as situations approach normalcy—don't wait for perfection. • Reduce your role as other roles require priority attention.

7

Student Development Openings

One of the most exciting things about working with youth in schools is that they are always changing. Physically, mentally, emotionally, and socially they evolve in a continual round of changes on their path from childhood to adulthood. It is easy to see how we need to adapt our interactions from the first grader to the high school senior, but the daily, weekly, and monthly changes are more difficult to recognize and react to appropriately. You have to depend on your experience, awareness, and the information previously presented to determine the most effective response for a given situation.

What follows are strategies that professionals have used to move students in productive academic and personal directions. To gain the most value from them, you must combine them with your personal style and energy along with an understanding of the hallways and what students need. The best results come from identifying your creative ways of implementing them or changing them into something different that fits you and students better.

AN ENCOURAGING WORD

There are appropriate situations for bad news to be presented. Those are the times and places in which people have the opportunity to feel sad, mad, or confused while not being pressed to have an immediately productive reaction. The place needs to be somewhere that negative reactions will not cause more problems than the discouraging news itself. There also needs to be time for initial reactions to be processed.

None of the conditions for presenting bad news are met in most hallway interactions. They are too brief and generally too public. The focus of hallway interactions needs to be on giving encouragement and support. All too often, however, people rushed and distracted in hallways can promote discouragement by their communication or lack of it. The following behaviors point out critical differences between being an encourager or a discourager.

Encouraging Communication	*Discouraging Communication*
Attentive and reflective listening	Hearing without confirming specific messages
Cooperative words and actions	Competitive or comparative to others
Accepting	Doubting, denying, rejecting, or threatening
Positives emphasized	Problem, mistake, or negative focus
Demonstrated interest in feelings	Avoidance of or nonreaction to feelings
Stimulating creative thinking	One way to think and be
Humor that communicates hope	Sarcasm and embarrassing humor
Appreciation of efforts and improvement	Recognition for final achievements only
Valuing the person	Valuing only performance

ACADEMIC THOUGHT ENCOURAGERS

Classroom learning and study at home are the principle ways students are expected to acquire the academic knowledge needed to demonstrate success. But what happens in between those times is a key source of knowledge that is often ignored. Why do math club members do better on math exams or those who work on the student newspaper do better on English tests? Why do students whose parents work in an academic field generally do well in those areas? Part of the answer is that these students spend time thinking and talking about specific areas when they are not in class or doing homework. They found sufficient interest and challenge to keep learning during nonrequired times. The challenge for educators is to find ways to keep that thinking going; ways that are interesting, challenging, and worthy of peer discussion.

Crossword Wall

What area of study deserves focus for the week? Have the teacher(s) focusing on that area come up with key words students will be studying and some hints. Any number of sites on the Web (just Google "create educational crossword puzzle") let you put in the words to create a hint and a puzzle.

Blow the puzzle up and put it on the wall in the hallway, lunchroom, or somewhere else where students congregate to make it highly noticeable. Put a box under the puzzle with an opening for students to write in the word that relates to the number on the puzzle. Write in the correct answers once before the end of the day so that students can look for what is left and talk with each other before they leave for home.

Lunch Lessons

Make up short games or puzzles around academic themes that would go on different tables at lunch. Not everyone will use them, but some will and that's a start. You can also expand the idea by adding contests for tables, classrooms, or teams to complete. Another option is for teachers to offer extra credit to groups who complete the task. The key is to make the tasks academic related, enjoyable, and encouraging of students working together.

CREATIVE COMMUNICATORS

Ideas are communicated in more than words. There are opportunities for students to explore academic, personal, and social communication in numerous ways. Here are two to start your thinking.

Sidewalk Expressions

Modern sidewalk chalk is a great medium for expression. Heavily used walkways generally get no notice, even though they have the potential to be wonderful message communicators. Sidewalk chalk is easy to use, environmentally friendly, and easy to clean up. Here are just a few ideas on how to use it:

- Geometric designs for math development
- Famous quotes related to subjects being studied or current celebrations
- Quizzes and questions to stretch thinking about areas of study
- Drawings for expressions of ideas
- Designs for nothing but their beauty

Signing Society

Everyone knows that signing is used for the deaf, but it also has the potential for many more uses. Learning any new language expands a person's view of communication and the world. It creates new ways to gain attention for ideas. Even when a group learns only a few signs, the tendency is to use and share them with others. When one or more educators in a school begins to share some thoughts by sign with students, others begin trying to learn in order to reciprocate. What evolves is a special sense to the communication that is uncommon, silent, and highly appropriate for hallway forms of communication.

Students already have many signs; some shared with adults and others not. A wave to say hello or head shakes to communicate yes or no are common in most cultures. Other signs are more culturally complex, like a handshake. A firm handshake can communicate positive strength or aggression depending on various mixtures of culture and gender. Some signs have much shorter histories and are more physical. High fives, low fives, butt bumps, and chest bumps have become common for enthusiastic greetings or congratulations. A wink, nod, or wiggle of a finger can all be signs between people when they don't want others to see. Signs are common to our communication, so experimenting with actual sign language has a natural human attraction as well as academic and social benefits.

Very little preparation and no real expertise is needed to make this work. Professionals can learn little by little and make mistakes right along with students. You don't need everyone to be involved, either. Start it yourself and invite other professionals and students as you try a few signs out with them. "Hello," "Good-bye," and "Thank you" are good starting places that you will find students matching your communication. The more participants advance (some will quickly surpass you if you are new), the greater will be opportunities for academic, personal, and social communication.

Wherever this communication leads, it will always be sparking different neurons in people's minds, which is great for all forms of development. It will also offer a new kind of interest around hallway interactions that extends learning beyond the classroom. The Easter Seal Society's *Friends Who Care Hearing Disabilities Worksheet* is a great starter poster. Start small and go no faster than is needed to draw people in to a new way of communicating.

Figure 7.1   Signing Tutorial

SOURCE: *Friends Who Care Program* published by Easter Seals. Reprinted by permission.

Purposeful Words

Once Americans traded the "King's English" for a more casual style of language, a degree of exactness was lost. We say things like "Think about why that happened," when we really mean "Analyze why that happened." The words "think about" don't suggest any particular model for how to think about an issue. "Analyze" on the other hand, communicates finding out about the parts of something and how they work together. One way to improve your hallway communication with students is to give more attention to the specific purpose of your message.

Bloom's Taxonomy (Bloom, 1984) is a classic model for specifying what type of cognitive operation is needed for a person to become a more effective thinker. It identifies six hierarchical operations ordered from the least to the most complex: Knowledge, comprehension, application, analysis, synthesis, and evaluation. Curricular development, educational research, the construction of tests (Kunen, Cohen, & Solman, 1981), and counselor supervision (Granello, 2000) have all been influenced by these concepts. Each of the six hierarchy levels provides an essential skill for acquiring information, and developing critical thinking.

Different educational practices can be designed to promote specific forms of learning based on Bloom's model. For example, sometimes we want students to be able to simply recall or recognize information (knowledge) about a behavior that is new to them, while other times we want them to combine pieces of information to come up with a new idea (synthesis) about how behaviors affect them. Developing understanding (comprehension) of how such a new behavior can be implemented is different from actually practicing (application) the new behavior. The Clarifying Communication Table follows the general descriptions based on those included in the Learning Skills Program (1999) and demonstrates the different areas of learning, the actions you would take to help someone acquire the information, what kind of action you are seeking from the student, and the process verbs to encourage responses for the learning desired. Consider a couple of examples of how this process worked during hallway interactions.

A third-grade math teacher was anxious about several of her students' ability to do simple multiplication. She thinks there is a need for some reinforcement and asks the counselor if she has any ideas for extra things that might help. Recognizing that this was little more than

(Continued)

(Continued)

straightforward knowledge recognition, the counselor asked for some copies of the teacher's flash cards to use.

She kept the cards with her and when she saw the students, she pulled out a flash card along with her smile and simply said, "Answer?" It took no more than seconds to do one or two cards and the conversation either continued to other things or they simply passed each other in the hallway with smiles. The game caught on and other teachers and students began playing quizzes as they passed each other in the hallway or at lunch.

Another counselor had a high school student struggling with whether to take a job in his father's shop after graduation or attend a college that would take him away from home. She ran into him at the local bowling alley and said, "Hi. How are you doing? Have you gotten any closer to a decision?"

"No," he said, "it is just too overwhelming to think about."

The counselor responded with a short statement that focused the student's attention on breaking the big decision into smaller pieces (analysis). "I can understand that. It's a big decision. I've found it valuable to start small by thinking of four things that affect the decision to see how each one would influence it. Maybe you could even write down something about them and share it?"

"Well maybe," He said. "If I do, can I ask you about it?"

"Sure. I'd be happy to talk more with you."

Both examples demonstrate reactions that were over in less than a minute. Knowledge practice was gained in one and an idea of how to analyze the problem was planted in another. Neither case promises a perfect result, but each provides a specific and appropriate interaction to stimulate a certain type of learning. The more your brief interactions clearly communicate the specific learning goal needed, the more timely and effective will be the assistance. You can use the Clarifying Communications Table to better select the tasks and words that match what you want someone to learn.

Figure 7.2 Clarifying Communication Via Bloom's Taxonomy

What You Are Trying to Develop in Someone	Hallway Helper Actions	Effective Student Responses	Process Verbs and Student Tasks	
Knowledge *(Remember or recognize specific information)*	directs tells shows examines	responds absorbs remembers recognizes	define repeat list name match identify show	memorize record relate label locate select collect
Comprehension *(Understand the information given)*	demonstrates listens questions compares contrasts examines	explains translates demonstrates interprets	restate describe explain identify report tell summarize report	discuss recognize express locate review rearrange group estimate
Application *(Use techniques, concepts, principles, & theories in new situations)*	shows facilitates observes criticizes	solves problem demonstrates use of knowledge constructs	translate apply employ practice illustrate sketch solve demonstrate	interpret dramatize operate schedule compute modify use

(Continued)

Figure 7.2 (Continued)

What You Are Trying to Develop in Someone	Hallway Helper Actions	Effective Student Responses	Process Verbs and Student Tasks
Analysis (Break complex ideas, concepts, or behaviors into their constituent elements or parts)	probes guides observes acts as a resource	discusses uncovers lists dissects	calculate appraise test diagram contrast compare criticize inspect debate inventory question relate solve examine analyze distinguish experiment outline differentiate separate infer subdivide
Synthesis (Original, creative thinking that forms a whole by putting constituent elements or parts together)	reflects extends analyzes evaluates	discusses generalizes relates compares contrasts abstracts	compose plan propose design formulate arrange assemble collect construct create set up organize manage prepare summarize write generate invent hypothesize modify

What You Are Trying to Develop in Someone	Hallway Helper Actions	Effective Student Responses	Process Verbs and Student Tasks	
Evaluation *(Develop & apply standards & criteria to judge the value of ideas, actions, & methods)*	clarifies accepts harmonizes guides	judges disputes develops criteria	judge evaluate compare score choose estimate measure support discriminate	appraise predict rate value select assess justify criticize rank

From Benjamin S. Bloom, *Taxonomy of Educational Objectives Book 1/Cognitive Domain*, 1st Ed., Published by Allyn & Bacon, Boston, MA. Copyright © 1984 by Pearson Education. Adapted by permission of the publisher.

MESSAGE MODELING

We are trained to model how educators, counselors, social workers, and administrators should act. That is a good starting place, but it doesn't model how a "student" should act. They are not in charge of others and don't have professional responsibilities on which to be held accountable. Modeling quality student behavior requires a look at what other aspects deserve to be modeled by any good member of a learning community.

Public Reading

Learners get much of their information from reading. How often do you carry a book or newspaper with you in the hallways, at lunch, or at an afterschool event? How often are you seen reading in public places? All too often we only do reading that stimulates our thinking in private or with family around. Educators are less likely to be seen reading novels, biographies, science magazines, or a major newspapers at school and therefore don't model such behaviors for students.

When you read something interesting while around others, you can share your interest directly. At the very least, those around see modeling of interest and learning, but it can also stimulate their interest in the topic. Conversations and follow-up actions may follow that all spur learning. The potential results come from hallway reading, but not from reading in isolation.

When students see you carrying reading material on a regular basis, sooner or later, some will ask what you are reading. They might become interested in the topic for its own sake or for its connection to you. But even if there is no interest and even if the students are not the ones to ask what you're reading, they see an adult who values books, reading, and information. So carry reading material and make yourself visible when reading. It has personal value for you as well as modeling how to be a learner for students.

Professional's Learning

Showing interest and talking with students about what they are learning is positive professional behavior. What it doesn't model is that we too are learners and excited about our own learning. I once worked with an educator for two year before finding out that he had become an avid reader of Civil War battles. He had no great agenda for the study other than to better understand and enjoy the learning. It was the joy of learning that helped me see him in a whole different light as a person and professional. It also encouraged me to think about my own learning and how much I enjoyed it when time was purposely set aside for it.

Students need to hear what adults in their lives are studying and learning. They need to see that learning is exciting, personally rewarding, and something that doesn't end when school is done. The message communicates the importance of learning for everyone and the fun of sharing what one is learning. It is the way we show students that their education is more than required tasks at this time in their lives, but instead a grand opportunity to learn and share what they are learning with others.

Whole Life Highlights

We are people before we are professionals just as youth are people before they are students. One of the reasons students often seek out each other out for guidance rather than professional educators is the desire to be understood as a person, which is much more complex than their student role. They know their peers will see them as a person first even when the issue is student related, because they have previously shared personal knowledge about themselves.

Professional educators who want to have the greatest impact on students need to share some of who they are as persons as well as who they are as professionals. Long detailed histories are not necessary or even wanted. It is brief information that shows you have a life outside of your professional role: a life that students can recognize as something with which they can identify.

The modeling of this behavior encourages students to share more of themselves as a natural part of many relationships. It demonstrates that the fears we all have of how much to share with others are often exaggerated and unnecessary. "If professionals I respect are not afraid of me knowing the more human and less perfect parts of their lives, then perhaps my fears and weaknesses might not be so bad and some could be opened for discussion with others." It is a healthier and more motivating model than never letting anyone see any part of us other than what a formal role requires.

Healthy Public Habits

Professionals drinking alcohol in school has been long eliminated, and tobacco is on its last legs there. We are at a time when incorporating healthy behaviors is even more important than eliminating obviously unhealthy ones. If we want students to lead healthier lifestyles, then we must model them.

Much of our healthier lifestyles would go on beyond the school day, but not all. What you eat for lunch and in between meals is important. Is it water or a sugary soft drink that you carry around during the day? You can generally judge how healthy you eat and drink during the school day, based on how publicly you do it. The more people of more types that you allow to see your habits, the more likely they are to be healthy.

Today's schools try to squeeze in as much learning time as possible, which makes healthy exercise a precious commodity. Afterschool activities are important in many ways, but modeling of healthy exercise within the school day is more of a challenge. Stretching works and it can be done is a wide variety of hallway situations. There are moments during the school day when there is a little extra time. Around lunchtime is usually one of these times. One teacher I knew always took five minutes at the end of the lunch period to go for a brisk walk. She did it outside if the day was clear and in the halls if it was not. She invited students and staff to go and she had a few consistent takers every day. What she also accomplished was to get others talking about it and, in many cases, talking about how they got their five minutes of exercise periodically during the school day. She rarely mentioned what she was doing; instead, it was the modeling that brought people onboard to take healthier steps.

AFFIRMATION STATEMENTS

What are the statements you make to affirm people and let them know they are doing well? Here are a few that may help expand your repertoire. Just add your own endings that are more specific to each student and your appreciation. Then integrate the ones you already use or develop as you go along.

Wow—neat!	Nice going.
All right—way to go!	Good thinking.
How did you do that?	You are really getting it now.
Thanks for bringing that up.	Neat idea.
Your opinion made a difference.	Thanks for helping.
That work is coming along well.	You've got it now.
I never thought of it that way.	Everyone's working hard.
You've made real progress.	Very interesting.
That's impressive effort.	You make it look easy.

8

Creating Adult
Opportunities

Adults are relatively equal in their freedom to do as they wish without legal control by others, which is very different from students. Educators have work responsibilities inside the school while parents and community members have similar obligations beyond school boundaries. These varied conditions call for adaptations to the actions we might use with students and elimination of others. They also require additional conceptualizing about how to encourage and get adults invested in the education of young people.

The activities in this chapter provide some starting places for thinking about how to gain the investment you want from adults. Those working inside the school certainly have more chances to deal with students, and your opportunities to interact with them are much greater. You will need to go a little further out of your way to influence parents and community members, but these efforts are valuable only to the degree you have the time and will to use the many opportunities that are present.

STAFF SUPPORTERS

A common factor in successful schools is that staff members feel good about work and can recognize that others support their efforts. These staff are more likely to go out of their way to help students or other staff members. They have a sense of power to make positive things happen and security in knowing that they will be supported in trying new things. When power, support, and enjoyment are common sensations for school staff, it operates more effectively, the climate is better for everyone, and students learn more. Developing this type of climate requires strategies that promote a sense of support, inclusion, and appreciation.

Food for Thought

Food has a significant impact on everyone, giving it an important place in developing productive relationships with adults in particular. It plays a significant social role in all cultures around the world as people physically come together for the communal experiences of eating. Commonalities are confirmed in the eating of traditional foods while cultural and personal uniqueness is explored through preferences. Then there are the simple comforts of food. Quieted hunger, the viewing of food that creates a positive expectation, a burst of flavor, a lingering taste, and the smell are all reminders of good things about life.

What follows are samples of ways professionals have used food to promote their relationships with staff members. It is important to remember that they should be personal actions and not things that the administration routinely does. They should communicate a sense of gifts and surprises rather than entitlements from official sources.

Pleasure Bowl

Start a trend by creating a pleasure bowl or tray for faculty and staff. It doesn't need to be expensive or particularly unique. Anything that attracts people's eyes, nose, or taste and can produce pleasure, a sense of importance, and a feeling of being cared about will work just fine. Place it in any common area where faculty and staff find themselves at one time or another during the day.

Sweets are, of course, the most common pleasure, but use your imagination and knowledge of staff members. You can have cultural days, healthy eating days, and sinfully pleasurable days or weeks. Holidays call for specially related treats. And don't forget to acknowledge those stressful times with foods that create a sense of peace during a hectic day.

Personalized Treats

Well-chosen food gifts are always valued by people who have done something for you or who need some special treatment. Two types of food gifts carry great personalized value in these situations. People often have special foods that are their particular treats and if you know them, you have the first type of special food identified. The other type of highly valued food gift is one that has a special story related to you or the gift. The more special and personal the story, the more it can be appreciated whether the recipients like the food or not.

Nonedible Gifts

Too much eating is not good for anyone, so a healthy gift climate needs to move beyond culinary joys alone. There are unlimited ways to give gifts and unlimited gifts to give. The only limit is the degree of understanding you have of the gift receiver's preferences and your own creative imagination. A few starters should get your creative juices flowing.

Floral Surprises

It is so easy to pick some free daffodils in the spring or stop for a simple $10 bouquet at the grocery store that we all ought to do it more regularly. This is particularly true in schools where people can be the only living things present.

Flowers in public places or as special gifts provide visual, smell, and touch sensations that help people step out of the mental and physical rush for short periods of time. They promote conversation, and you don't need to have them available all the time. They are wonderful treats when they are special. So bring them on an irregular basis and you'll find that they are appreciated even more.

Birthday Acknowledgments

Birthdays are generally good times to acknowledge someone in a simple, yet meaningful way. A card, flower, doughnut, chocolate bar, or cup of coffee delivered with no fanfare shows caring without the hassle of a big celebration. Most adults appreciate this type of subdued acknowledgment more than something showy. The older we get, the truer this becomes, as concerns about age creep into our consciousness.

Support Simplicity

We all run into difficult times and one of the problems during those times is that people want to tell you how bad they feel for you. The result is that the person who has lost a loved one, developed an illness, separated from a partner, or is struggling in some other aspect of his or her life feels the need to give comfort rather than be comforted. So make your support gifts simple ones that show attention and availability rather than trying to make things better.

One more guiding principle is to not communicate, "I know how you feel." Let the people have their own feelings and if they come to you because they sense you can help, great. But if you are not the one they need, then you've done them a great favor by not pushing yourself on them.

Mystery Arrivals

Like random acts of kindness, gifts that come from no one at no particular time generate thoughts, smiles, appreciation, wonder, and conversation about why this nice thing happened and from whom it came. The pleasures aren't limited to the person receiving the gift, but extend to everyone who becomes part of the conversations. Use these to put a little enjoyable mystery into the life of a school when things can get awfully routine, by February and March in particular.

On-Time Appearances

Helpers like to say, "I'm here for you" or "I'm ready to help with this project," but the words aren't necessarily taken as the whole truth. The words communicate an idea, but it is actions that communicate the full truth. There is probably no better gift for a person in need of support with a personal issue, professional problem, or task that needs to be done than for someone to be physically present exactly when needed.

Being where you are expected when you are expected, or being at the right time and place to help when you are not expected is huge in making a person feel supported and increasing the chances of something new and positive occurring. It promotes both quality task accomplishment and relationship building. When you come five minutes late, you have made one or more people more anxious than they needed to be. You are a relief at five minutes late, but outstanding when on time. The more important the situation is to someone, the greater difference your on-time behavior will make in the quality of the meeting.

No one is on time all the time. People are delayed for various reasons and sometimes we just forget. These are not excuses but, instead, the reasons why being on time as often as humanly possible makes a significant difference in the overall climate of a school and the relationships among staff members. The principal will take the opinion of the person who is consistently present at the appointed meeting time in a more positive light than that of others whose only difference is that they are regularly late. The teacher who needs help with a physically challenged student arriving at 10:30 will look for ways to support and reward the professional who is there at 10:25. People appreciate timeliness in others even when they are not good at it themselves. Success, relationships, and climate are improved when people are on time. The one person you can start with is yourself.

Borrowed Gifts

Remember the last time someone asked to borrow something that had particular meaning to you? Perhaps it was a book, a lesson plan you developed, a special recipe, or a handout you got in a workshop that was very meaningful to you. The feelings are pride and appreciation that someone values my work or something that is important to me. Borrowing something from someone hardly sounds like a traditional gift, but when done appropriately, it conveys much the same message: "You are valued by me."

These are particularly meaningful gifts to adults working in busy schools. "Of course, you know I value what you do" is the thought that gets in the way of actually showing someone his or her value. Even the direct verbal messages of "Thank you" and "You do a good job" only communicate value in an abstract form. When you ask to share and care for something of another person, it validates a piece of who they are and what they believe.

There are warnings that go with borrowing:

Be sure that the other person sees what you ask for as valuable.

Clearly state your appreciation with assurances that you will return it in perfect condition.

Set a specific time to return it and then be sure to return it on time and in perfect condition.

Returning something borrowed allows additional opportunities for hallway helping. Verbal appreciation is, of course, required, but don't make it too flowery. Too much sounds fake. Perhaps you have something that has some relationship to what was borrowed and could add to the person's thinking— a book, a handout, a reference, or a recipe of your own. It is an additional opportunity to give a piece of you back that can be further appreciated. Borrowing done well demonstrates valuing of others in multiple ways while also directly supporting relationship development and the expansion of ideas outside one's limited viewpoint.

Idea Expanders

People don't suddenly go from inside-the-box thinkers to creative thinkers. They don't change negative thinking patterns to positive ones in a single swift decision. People need to be encouraged to think creatively and positively on a regular basis. You know the feeling when you've been involved in a workshop or seminar and come out enthusiastically ready for change only to have the enthusiasm dry up when no one else will engage with you in the exciting thinking and new actions. Enthusiasm, motivation, creativity, and willingness to try new things need to become a part of a pattern in a school or community so that one person encourages another.

You can start the encouragement of thinking new and positive thoughts in a number of ways. Rarely do these methods require any long discussions. Actually, the more you talk about something new for the first time with someone, the more likely you are to turn them off. What works better is to initiate ideas and motivation with bits and pieces of special information. The following are a few examples.

Quick Tips

If you are like most people, you pick up a newsletter and first read the short pieces and particularly those that offer health, beauty, or professional tips. It is a busy world with so much information it can be overwhelming. Find a short idea that helps you do something more effectively or efficiently or with more pleasure and it feels like you have moved forward. It is growth and relief of pressure all in one small piece.

We generally don't go looking for tips for ourselves, but we appreciate it when they come to us in a less-than-30-second-per-tip reading format. The Internet has made tip finding remarkably easy. Just Google any term on your computer, along with the word tips, and you'll find plenty of options: history tips, health tips, parenting tips, discipline tips, diet tips, writing tips, and tips for dealing with difficult people. Success in expanding people's thinking with tips requires presenting them in small doses.

You can get tips to people individually when you know someone who is looking to expand ideas on an issue or problem. Give people one or two tips that you think fit and see what they think. Their response will tell you if they want more tips (send them to the Web site), to talk more about them (conversation starter), or if they are not much interested right now (the tips are in their hands to use if and when they do need them). No matter the result, if you take up a minimum amount of their time, you will have expanded their thinking and demonstrated positive feelings for them.

You can also create tips that focus on general issues in a school such as health, learning, discipline, creative projects, or testing. The longer the list of tips you create, the less anyone will read them! So the task is to give out just a few from time to time to everyone, with only three to six tips at one time. This can focus discussion among the staff that can lead to individuals benefiting from a specific tip, creative new ideas originating from them, and sometimes even group planning for how to do things differently. Any of these results puts the school and the staff ahead of where they were and moving in a positive direction.

Web and Book Highlights

So much information is available and so much more is coming every day that we can't keep up with it. Most of us relegate ourselves to a select number of information sources determined by what we know, where we look, and how hard we look. You can help an individual or whole school staff by offering Web sites and books that could be particularly helpful. Teachers might be interested in academic puzzle creation, lesson plan ideas, bulletin board topics, specialty supplies, or how to keep calm when stress is high.

All you need to do is select a topic and take 20 minutes to do a Google search. You can also pass the topic around to people and see what they have found most helpful. Once you have a couple of good sites or books, you can send them around to people with an "I found this helpful" note or post them on a *Web site and Book Tips* bulletin board. They don't need to be used by everyone, but the expansion of thinking for some will eventually rub off on others and any such growth improves the individual, the school, and student education.

Self-Seeking Support

Generally we help others expand their thinking by giving them an idea or resource. There is another way to do it and communicate trust and confidence at the same time: *ask for ideas.* Everyone from the principal, to teachers, lunch workers, and bus drivers are flattered when asked for ideas. It demonstrates belief in the quality of their ideas and the knowledge or skills they have. Even when they don't have any ideas for what we request, it will be taken as a compliment, particularly by those that we don't interact with on a daily basis.

The best way to do this is to know enough about the individual to have a sense that they can provide some type of positive input. The bus driver will definitely have ideas on "What do you find most useful in dealing with discipline and what have you tried that doesn't work?" The math teacher will appreciate being asked about "What numbers or statistics might best show the data I've collected on our career development program?" But there will also be a particular teacher who will be flattered and interested in talking more about "How can I get my roses to stay hearty over several years?"

The best questions to flatter people, get them thinking about their own work, how to improve it, and what's best for students and the school are the ones that fit that person. The better you know the person beyond his or her professional role, the greater success you will have with motivating the person by asking for ideas.

PARENTAL PARTNERSHIPS

My experience of how much parents mean to an effectively functioning school and the academic, career, and personal development of students begins with a memory from 50 years ago as a grade-school student.

I was in sixth grade in Woodrow Wilson Elementary School in Neptune City, New Jersey. Several of us boys were outside after lunch teasing Nancy about her weight. Minutes later, another girl told us that Nancy was going to tell the teacher. We panicked! No, it wasn't what the teacher would do. It was that our mothers were likely to find out what we had done!

My Mom was a member of the Fire Auxiliary and a bowling league, both of which included teachers. She was always coming home knowing something about what was going on at school and who was behaving in what ways. It was that way for all of us. Our parents knew the teachers, administrators, and board members as adults with things in common. Their personal sense of each other created trust and cooperation.

We apologized and begged Nancy not to tell. It was embarrassing, but she didn't tell and we didn't get in trouble. The memory is so strong that it must have been a powerful lesson for me.

That long-ago event is a continual reminder of how important it is to create a sense of person-to-person connection with parents in addition to the professional-to-parent relationship. The more small things we can do to foster those relationships the better.

Connecting Questions

There are questions that make parents uncomfortable with educators and the schools whereas other questions help them feel connected. Most of the time when we connect with parents it is about some issue with their child, so they come feeling anxious, defensive, or sometimes angry. Before you get to the hard questions, there are others that can communicate interest in the whole of the parent and not just the issue of concern. They are the type of questions that show you as more than a professional; you are additionally someone not so different from himself or herself. Using questions wisely can make cooperation much more likely.

Family Portraits

People like professionals to show personal interest in positive aspects of their families. One or two initial questions can communicate that with very little time taken up. You might ask, "How many children do you have?" or, "Where is Ellen in relation to your other children?"

Simple current family questions can create opportunities to briefly reflect on the answers by showing something of yourself: "I came from a family of three also. It seemed to work for me," or if your situation was very different, "I was an only child and always wished there were brothers and sisters. Do you find that it would make a difference?"

Family Evolution

A history of one's family can provide another opportunity to start a conversation in a personal way. There are many questions that can be answered briefly and still initiate conversation. For example, "Warren mentions visiting with grandparents. Do you have other family around?"

A father might reply, "Yes, our parents live about 20 miles away and we see them a couple times a month."

This would give you the opportunity to say something about yourself in connection with a little more exploration of their family history, origins, and travels. Remember that this is less about gaining information, and more about developing a relationship. The more you pursue these questions as support for some type of prevention or intervention for a child, the less you will be developing the personal connection. Keep discussion short and connect the comments to yourself if you want to develop a personal relationship that will lead to stronger partnerships.

Fashion Statements

The first interaction people have when they meet in person is visual. We see each other and quickly identify similarities and differences. When those meeting have something about them that is similar and something else that is a little different, it makes for a good conversation starter. To use this tactic, you might think about what you are wearing and pay attention to the other person's apparel.

Hair, skin color, and body size are not the types of things you can change very easily about yourself. Rings, watches, pins, shirts, and shoes can be adjusted a little more easily. What might attract the interest of a man versus a woman? How might individuals from rural, suburban, and inner-city environments react differently? What fits with Asian-American, African-American, or an international culture? The idea is not to dress exactly like the other person, since this will look phony. The effort is to wear something that the other person might identify with that also says something about you as a person.

The second way to consider dress is recognizing what you might comment on about the other person. Jewelry, clothes, and hairstyles offer potential opportunities here as well. The important point to keep in mind is that comments about another person's looks need to be kept at a mild level. Too much interest or enthusiasm can turn a person off. Comments of this type would generally be very brief, but they can show that you are interested in the individuality of a person.

My experience is that women are generally better and more comfortable at this than men, but everyone can make some progress here. Just keep your eyes open, and occasionally you will see something that you feel comfortable commenting on that fits the person, the situation, and yourself.

Community Participation

People often have community roles in which they take pride. Asking a question or two in this area to promote a relationship takes knowing a little something about the person. The mother who coaches a soccer team will love a question about her involvement as much as the father who works with Special Olympics, or the grandparents who volunteer at the library. The idea that you care about these aspects of their lives enough to know them in the first place and seek to know them better helps you cement a personalized cooperative relationship.

Work Works

People generally feel like their employment is understood and appreciated by those similarly employed, but not by those outside that area. This is particularly true when a college-educated person is interacting with a person who has less formal education. Showing genuine interest in a person's work can be particularly productive in relationships with those whose types of work are very different in some way from yours.

The most relationship-productive work questions reflect interest in the work itself, whereas asking what job a person holds can be counterproductive. This question sends the message we are looking for a label, like sanitary engineer, lawyer, house-husband, mechanic, or grocery store clerk. The reaction on people's faces generally communicates the concern, "And how will you judge me now?" The questioner falls immediately into a judgment hole, which is not where you want to start.

Better work-related questions demonstrate interest in the activities of the other's work. We find it easier to identify productive questions for some types of work than others based on our biases. Most educators could find interest in the work of a structural engineer, for example: "You must do a lot of computer work on models, but how hard is it to then translate that into real materials and structures?" But there are many more jobs that are very different from our general experiences and these are the ones for which potential connections can be most important.

It might seem hard to find a question for a sanitary engineer (trash collector), but there is still opportunity for relationship-development questions. "When my trash is picked up on Monday morning, there is a sensation of relief and cleanliness around the house. Do you get any sense of people's appreciation as you collect?" The key task is to get beyond our personal biases about work to see the value and importance of work that is very different from our own. When people sense a person's true interest in the experience of their work, they begin to see that person as someone worthy of their cooperative involvement.

Coffee Club

When the national media wants to focus on how the general population thinks about national or local issues, they go to the local diner for interviews. Diners and coffee shops are among the last remaining places where people gather to talk on a regular basis. People spend time in large homes and spacious back decks, which allow for privacy, rather than on front porches, but what we lose are the everyday connections with neighbors and the community beyond family and work. Educators can make some of those connections by dropping in on the places where people gather for something to drink and a bite to eat around their workday.

Morning Coffee

One way I can settle myself before beginning a day at the office is to get out of the house, where projects are always calling, and stop for a a cup of coffee before getting to the office where work demands my attention. A stop at a McDonald's to enjoy a cup of coffee, read the paper, and say hello to the morning group that comes and goes is more than a respite. It is a time when someone can stop to ask about his or her child, the school, or simply recognize me. I can do the same as I learn who the regular patrons are. Noneducators enjoy the idea that an educator would spend a little time in their neighborhood, because it is not the norm and demonstrates respect and commonality.

The place to stop when I worked as a counselor in rural Idaho was the Hanson Honda Shop. People gathered there before the workday for a cup of coffee. Everyone would chip in or bring some coffee, tea, or juice so there was always plenty any time of day. It was the place to learn the local news and solidify the connection between the school and the mostly farming community. Never did I work in a place that was more supportive of my actions and the actions of the schools.

The key is to locate the places where people gather to relax and talk. You don't need to be in the conversation groups to gain credibility, information, and support. Mostly you just need to show up once in a while.

Lunch With the Counselor

Administrators often join the local Rotary Club or something similar to establish relationships with the community. Several counselors and school psychologists I've known have done that as well, but it seems to be somewhat of a duplication to meet with the same people. One technique that taps into different parent populations is setting up a weekly or once-per-month "Lunch with the Counselor/Teacher" opportunity. It can be arranged in the school, but is generally more productive in a local casual establishment where parents would be more likely to feel at ease.

You will find that local casual restaurants like to have this connection. It is good for business. They are generally agreeable to putting up a notice that the counselor, history teacher, or third-grade teacher will be in on Friday at lunchtime, from

11:30 to 12:30, to eat and chat about school. The goal is not to create a large audience, but to demonstrate the accessibility of you and the school to parents and the general public. It is key to keep the conversation light and not let it run overtime. You are developing relationships, not solving problems.

A question that always comes up is how the school gets along if one of the staff is out of the school building for an hour or two. This is one strategy that needs a little support from administrators and colleagues, but the results are very worthwhile.

Parent Recreation

There are events worth attending periodically in which parents are relaxed and playing their chosen parts in the community. Celebrations and athletic events are particular situations during which you can improve relationships with parents by doing little more than being there. The parents will appreciate seeing you in their leisure world and respect you if you are enjoying yourself in environments similar to theirs.

Kids' Day

One of the traditions many towns have started are days set aside for kids to enjoy. Sometimes they are the official Kids' Day celebration in the early fall, but they go by various other local titles. The model for these days is lots of activities to involve children and of course lots of food. Everyone is focused on children and the family, so what better community event is there for a school professional to be part of than this?

Some people are good at mixing and starting conversations with people at these events. I, however, am not one of those people, and need to have a role to feel comfortable enough to make conversation. Without a role, I'll just walk around, make some face-to-face contact and feel uncomfortable the whole time. I'm still seen and appreciated for being there, but it is a struggle for me. So my personal tactic is to find a role beforehand, by volunteering to help at any of the events or food stands. Once I have something to do, I can then talk to anyone.

> *The key is to know yourself well enough to decide how to make the event work for you, remembering that just being there for a short while will increase your credibility with the community and parents.*

Celebrations come in many forms, but they almost always have something for parents and children. It is particularly worthwhile to keep an eye out for those organized by local churches. These are not likely to be the largest events and that makes them more valuable for making connections. You will also come in contact here with many people you rarely, if ever, see at school. Minorities who often feel disassociated from schools tend to have strong religious ties that give these events added importance. The connections you make can wind up being particularly strong, because of the highly personal nature of church affiliations. If you can get yourself to just two or three events a year, you will gain acceptance and investment from community members that cannot be earned inside the school.

Little Leaguers

Baseball, basketball, soccer, and even junior football games are all great places to be seen and connect with parents. The events that focus on the children often attract different groups of parents, depending on the event. Those whose children are in soccer are often different from those whose children play junior football, so you can see different groups in places that fit them best.

It is not all traditional athletics. There are dance recitals, gymnastic meets, swimming meets, and more opportunities. Each one presents the chance to be seen as a professional interested in the whole lives of children rather than only their academic side. Of course, the benefits here also extend to connections with the students, who take great pride in a counselor's or teacher's interest in them beyond the school and academic boundaries. Your stock will rise with both parents and adults.

Adults Play, Too

Connecting with parents is not all about what kids do. Parents also have their athletic and cultural forms of entertainment from which they derive personal joy and pride. Showing interest in these activities creates a more adult-to-adult level of involvement that has in a different kind of power from when the parent-professional relationship is focused on the child's activities.

Adults play sports too, though not as many or as often as their children. Softball, baseball, soccer, and flag football are played by many adult males with school-age children. Mothers who play can also be found, but certainly not as many. You get to understand a person better when you can see them in competitive events. Team events offer particular insights into what types of interactions are productive with them and what ones are not.

Sporting events are not the only places to interact with parents around their personal leisure activities. Parents also play in community bands or at the jazz club in town. Some love karaoke and others can be found at bridge tournaments or selling their wares at arts and crafts shows. They are pleased about what they do, and when you show up they are impressed with your interest. "This is a person who can appreciate what I like and do."

9

Daily Positive Messages

Every day you spend at school as well as those times you spend interacting in the community you are sending messages. The first message shouts, "I am here!" It is few words but a giant statement. You have made a decision to be present in the lives of specific people while multitudes of others have chosen not to be there. You enter a small minority of positive influencing people in someone's life, and that potential needs to be used in productive ways on a continuing basis.

Selectively chosen words and specific actions are the primary communicators of hallway helping, but each day you communicate in multiple ways. Your message of being in the hallway (visible and involved) is different for most people from the one you give when you are in the office (invisible and involvement unknown). A smile (positive) says something different from a frown (angry? troubled? worried?). What you communicate day-to-day and throughout the day will vary based on the situations and your reactions to them. Continuing to communicate positive messages requires that you attend to all the ways in which you communicate. This final chapter offers some positive communication ideas to carry with you throughout your hallway helping interactions.

BODY TALK

There is a stage in horse training referred to as the "join up," when a horse has decided that it doesn't want to fight or run from the trainer any more. It wants to be a part of the trainer's world and work in partnership. The horse shows it by licking its lips and lowering the head. When the skilled trainer recognizes the behavior, she breaks direct eye contact, turns her back to the horse, and slowly walks away. If the horse is fully ready, it will follow and put its head close to the trainer when she stops. The partnership is identified and sealed without a word being spoken.

Body language is the key tool for horse trainers who choose to forgo more harsh and demanding methods. It is based on the fact that horses are social creatures and want partnership more than isolation. Without the ability to use words, they have developed their own methods of nonverbal communication and much of it is through body language.

Human beings are also very social beings, and even though we have evolved a remarkably sophisticated verbal language, our body language still tells a great deal about us. We are so caught up in words that our tendency is to ignore the value of body messages, but they are there nevertheless and continue to affect relationships. What follows are a few essential aspects of body talk that greatly add to our understanding of people in the hallway and our ability to communicate effective messages.

Stance Messages

June was a school counselor trainee who was doing a fifth-grade guidance presentation when I was making a supervision visit. She had a solid plan, but I knew she would be in trouble as soon as I saw her step to the head of the class. She stood ramrod straight, feet together, in the exact middle of the front of the room, and looked just over the heads of the students. The students almost immediately began talking together, drawing, or daydreaming. She lost their attention almost before she was started.

The posture that June took was very similar to what would be called "attention" in the military. In fact, that form of attention (ramrod straight, feet tight together, arms at the sides, and looking straight ahead) can be found in any formal military organization in the past fifteen centuries! The position communicates obedience and defenselessness to a superior. Without thinking, something in June's students let them know that she was not in control.

Control Stance

Standing tall needs to be combined with a forward lean, one foot forward, and arms forward to communicate self-confidence, control, and strength. This is the ready position that any athlete or soldier would take, and it communicates much the same thing for educators. In the hallways it lets people know that you are confident being in a situation, attentive to things around you, and able to help as needed.

Power Height

We can't all be the tall dark handsome type, but we can communicate different aspects of power by how we use the height we do have. Put yourself in a position looking down on someone, and you communicate that you are taking strong control. We learn this at the earliest ages by recognizing that everyone who controls us towers over us. It takes a long time to get over that sense that height means power and control, and we often come to resent it. This position should be used only when you want to assert your control most forcefully.

Why do counselors sit in chairs with clients and get on their knees to play with young children? The simple answer is that we want to give a sense of equality to the relationship. Putting yourself on the same level as another person creates an unstated equality that allows opportunities for more collaboration than a power position.

Sometimes we want the other person to feel strong and take control of a conversation or situation rather than seek our guidance. These are the times when we might take a position that put us just a little bit lower than the other person. A quick conversation with a student on a step and you sitting, or a student sitting and you taking a kneeling position are simple examples. Just reducing your posture a little can give the same effect.

Power Height

Above	Level	Below
Taking power and control	Equal power and control	Give away power and control

Look Influence

People pay more attention to you when you pay attention to them. The better you can match your directional look to the personal, situational, and cultural needs, the more casual influence you will create for yourself.

Close Attention

A straight-on look into someone's eyes lets them know that you are paying very close attention to them . . . whether they want it or not. If people want that direct look it is very positive, but if they are uncomfortable with it the look will communicate a desire to control them. You use this look when the person wants and can accept your most direct attention or when you need to give that direct attention to demonstrate how serious you feel a situation is.

Relaxed Attention

A less powerful look is one that goes off to the side of a person. It can communicate deference to the person, thoughtfulness, or even lack of attention, depending on the situation and person. What it will do is show that you are still with the person, but at a lower and less personally pressured level. It is a useful look for communication when the other individual or group has some degree of hesitancy about sharing information or being involved in the interaction.

Presence-Only Attention

Even facing away from someone can communicate attention. It is certainly not direct attention, but when a person knows you are there and attentive in general, they will act differently than if you weren't there at all. You don't require them to attend to you, but at the same time you are present. Just being close can be enough to show you are part of a person's world, and this can be supportive or prevent a problem situation from getting worse.

Eye Pressure

Much like the direction you are facing, how long you hold eye contact communicates the level of attention you are giving. Continuing to hold direct eye contact over time creates a very intense and personal connection that is often overpowering. The frequency and period of time that you shift eye focus away from the other individual's eyes creates psychological space and breathing room. How much room you and the other person want or need is the determining factor in how to proceed. It is not hard to determine when the other person wants more space, because he or she will physically move away or increasingly look somewhere other than directly at you.

Dress Connections

What you decide to wear can be more than personal preference. You can use subtle or large differences in how you dress to increase the potential to connect with a specific individual or group. One counselor always seemed to wear something unique to her personal look while at the same time fitting into the general look of those around her. I mentioned it to her one day and she let me know her very clear reasoning.

> *"I've found that parents, students, teachers, and administrators all react to me more positively if I'm wearing something they can identify with as similar to their style. They also like a little something unique. Sometimes women or children, but rarely men, will ask about what I'm wearing or my hairstyle, but mostly they just react more positively if I've picked something that fits them. So I try to take on a look for the day that is as similar as possible to what I think will be pleasant to the people I'll focus on in a given day or meeting, but which also has something that feels unique to who I am."*

I have no sense of dress and clothing like this counselor, nor do I have one hundredth of her wardrobe. But even for a simple dresser like myself there are some categories of dress that can be taken into account. If you want to demonstrate that you are comfortable and ready to interact with those in formal power, then you dress along more formal lines. Administrators, business people, legislators, and board members generally fit into this category, so these are people with whom I would put on a tie and maybe a jacket or even my one suit depending on the situation. This is my formal expert dress, which I wear as infrequently as I can.

Relaxed casual would be the term I'd use to describe my style, so it's good that I like counselors and schools because they allow for a less formal and more comfortable dress that fits me reasonably well. My dress tries to promote acceptance without calling any great attention to it. Mostly, I like a look that communicates equality and allows other aspects of my character to become the focus.

Then there are times when you want to communicate uniqueness. It's the dress-up day at school or the community celebration of Kids' Day. This is the time to look different in ways that bring you some attention and demonstrate you are not afraid to be different. Another of those times can be when you wear old jeans and a tee shirt at an event where that kind of dress is common. You can see the message reflected in people's eyes, a smile, and sometimes stated directly by students, "I've never seen you like that before!" This is the kind of dress that shows you are person like other people and not just a professional. The idea adds a whole new dimension to relationships and your acceptance into these students' world.

Consistency and Variety

One overall consideration with how your body talks is the consistency and variety of your messages and how they are received. People actually require both consistency and variety for a healthy existence and development. We all need a certain level of confidence in what to expect in order to make reasonable judgments about what actions to take. Knowing what stores carry the food or clothes we need at prices we can afford frees us from worry about going without. But we also get excited when the new store opens or our favorite stores have a special sale.

> *Consistency provides the stability and comfort that allows us to focus on other issues and variety provides the flexibility and creative potential for adding something new to our lives.*

Whether it is body movement, eye contact, facial expressions, or dress, those we want to help need both consistency and variety from us. Consistency tells them what to expect from us on a day-to-day basis. They know what we can offer and that it will be there for them when needed. When people can also see that we are not stagnantly consistent, but have interesting variations to our thoughts and behaviors, we communicate the potential for new growth and adventure.

People need to see professionals when they are sad, tired, and not so motivated in order to appreciate the upbeat and hopeful persona they see on a regular basis. Everyone experiences down times, worries, frustrations, and failures. When those we touch on a consistent basis are never shown these parts of ourselves, they lose the productive sense of reality that helps them evaluate themselves. Personal relationship is lost and only the surface professional remains.

We are in the business of helping people change and grow. To be good models for growth and change, we must demonstrate our own needs and changes in some aspect of the relationship. There are unlimited ways of doing it by physically acting different, changing our dress style, or just showing an expression that isn't expected. Each variation from our consistent presentation creates interest about who we are and how we live our lives. That interest brings people to us personally and professionally as long as they know that the consistent professional will also be there for security.

BIG IDEAS IN FEW WORDS

Not all messages come from you directly. Some messages are planted where others will connect with them. Quotations are an example. They show up on a wall, a paperweight, a calendar, a shirt, or in a newsletter. They are powerful when they are directly connected to a current issue or theme in a person's life. They tap something important inside us with only a few words to reinforce ideas and behaviors.

The hallway secret to using quotes is in the planting. Just like in a garden, you can't do the growing yourself. Your task in both cases is to identify the right place to plant, the best season for planting, the conditions needed for growth, and then adapt your actions as the factors change. The plants and conditions then do the work while you wait and watch. The tasks are similar for planting hallway quotes:

- *Find the right places* where quotes will likely to be recognized by those who need to see them. It could be the hallway for general consumption, your office door for people walking by, the door to the math class before a major test, or the gymnasium to emphasize sportsmanship as well as winning. Put the same message in the wrong place and it has no impact.

- *Select quotes that support the key themes being taught* that need reinforcement. The value of scientific procedures, the importance of appropriate wording, the benefits of understanding economics, or the essential skills of reading are examples of the many academic themes that can benefit from reinforcement of student work in these areas.

- *Match quotes to the conditions people are experiencing.* The tensions around standardized testing periods, anxieties heightened by bullying among students or staff, the need for extra effort and motivation around the middle of a long school year, the enthusiasm at the beginning of the year, or the trauma of a school tragedy each calls for quotes that can help focus people's thinking in productive ways.

- *Change the focus,* since needs for support and growth do not remain constant. What is a great quote at one time and place seems irrelevant at others. Great quotes remain great quotes, but they don't maintain their power for people over time. They need to be changed to reignite motivation and enthusiasm.

Finding quotes to match the needs of people has become remarkably simple with the Internet. All you need to do is Google the words or phrases for which you want quotes and the Internet will lead you there quickly. Of course, a myriad of books are also available for finding the right quotes for your needs. I try to collect quotes for myself, although in a rather haphazard way. But even with this unstructured collection model, I've gathered many over the years and offer just a few of my favorites to stir your thinking.

Strength and Courage

I always wondered why somebody doesn't do something about that. Then I realized I was somebody.

—Lily Tomlin

Aerodynamically a bumblebee shouldn't be able to fly, but the bumblebee doesn't know that so it goes on flying anyway.

—Mary Kay Ash

In the end, we will remember not the words of enemies, but the silence of our friends.

—Martin Luther King, Jr.

Courage is what it takes to stand up and speak; Courage is also what it takes to sit down and listen.

—Winston Churchill

Growth and Struggle

Smooth seas do not make good sailors.

—African proverb

Mistakes are the usual bridge between inexperience and wisdom.

—Phyllis Theroux

Difficulties mastered are opportunities won.

—Winston Churchill

There are no secrets to success. It is the result of preparation, hard work, and learning from failure.

—General Colin Powell

When defeat comes, accept it as a signal that your plans are not sound. Rebuild those plans and set sail once more toward your coveted goal.

—Napoleon Hill

The gem cannot be polished without friction, nor man perfected without trials.

—Chinese proverb

We're all ignorant, just on different subjects.

—Will Rogers

A ship in harbor is safe—but that is not what ships are for.

—John A. Shedd

Education and Learning

By failing to prepare, you are preparing to fail.

—Benjamin Franklin

Whether you believe you can do a thing or not, you are right.

—Henry Ford

Education is for improving the lives of others and for leaving your community and world better than you found it.

—Marian Wright Edelman

The mediocre teacher tells. The good teacher explains. The superior teacher demonstrates. The great teacher inspires.

—William Arthur Ward

Tell me . . . and I forget. Teach me . . . and I learn. Involve me . . . and I remember.

—Benjamin Franklin

Change is Necessary

Change is the only constant in life. One's ability to adapt to those changes will determine your success in life.

—Benjamin Franklin

Be the change you want to see in the world.

—Mahatma Gandhi

Not everything that is faced can be changed, but nothing can be changed until it is faced.

—James Baldwin

Impacting Others

They may forget what you said, but they will never forget how you made them feel.

—Carol Buchner

I will permit no man to narrow and degrade my soul by making me hate him.

—Booker T. Washington

You can make more friends in two months by becoming more interested in other people than you can in two years by trying to get people interested in you.

—Dale Carnegie

Do not wait for leaders; do it alone, person to person.

—Mother Teresa

Never believe that a few caring people can't change the world. For, indeed, that's all who ever have.

—Margaret Mead

The smallest good deed is better than the grandest good intention.

—Duguet

That old law about an eye for an eye leaves everyone blind.

—Martin Luther King, Jr.

You can't stay in your corner of the forest waiting for others to come to you. You have to go to them sometimes.

—Winnie the Pooh

There is no exercise better for the heart than reaching down and lifting people up.

—John Andrew Holmes

Work and Career

Find out what you like doing best and get someone to pay you for doing it.

—Katherine Whitehorn

I'm a great believer in luck, and I find the harder I work the more I have of it.

—Thomas Jefferson

I've missed more than 9000 shots in my career. I've lost almost 300 games. 26 times I've been trusted to take the game winning shot and missed. I've failed over and over and over again in my life. And that is why I succeed.

—Michael Jordan

Analyzing what you haven't got as well as what you have is a necessary ingredient of a career.

—Orison Swett Marden

What is the recipe for successful achievement? To my mind there are just four essentials:

Choose a career you love, give it the best there is in you, seize your opportunities, and be a member of a team.

—Benjamin F. Fairless

Three rules of work:

Out of clutter find simplicity; From discord find harmony; In the middle of difficulty lies opportunity.

—Albert Einstein

FINAL REMINDERS

Once you have the training and experience to be an effective professional, helping in the hallways becomes a matter of using skills consistently and reflexively in places where your training didn't guide you. Plying those skills outside the office and classroom will not be in the job description, but doing so carries benefits beyond those available in official work locations. This book has offered the critical constructs, process, and some initial strategies to get you started. Now your creative ideas, initiative, and follow through are all that is left. As you work your ways in the hallways, take time to reflect on a few basic concepts to maintain focus on what you are doing as a hallway helper, why you are doing it, and the pleasures that are there for you:

- *More contacts mean more productive opportunities*—The more positive brief contacts you make with people related to the school, the more you can change uninvolved bystanders into helpful contributors. The most productive and supportive school environments are those that continuously involve more and more people as contributors to the health of the school community.
- *Use the time you have*—Most of your day is spent outside your office already. Hallway helping is simply a better way of using that time and those places.
- *Schedules and rules work for you*—Schedules and rules of schools tell you where people are and what they will be doing. This organization allows you to plan for even the most casual of encounters throughout the day.
- *Take small steps and multiple opportunities*—You don't have to get it all done at once. The multiple and unending nature of potential hallway helping opportunities allows for the use of goals and actions that are limited in duration and scope, developmental, and flexible enough to change over time.

- *No need to be perfect, so be creative and enjoy*—More than enough low-impact hallway opportunities are available to allow for innovative strategies and making up for mistakes you might make. Final outcomes are not riding on each interaction, so relax a little and enjoy your hallway experiences. They are always there waiting for you.

References and Suggested Readings

Blanchard, K., & Johnson, S. (1982). *The one-minute manager.* New York: William Morrow.

Bloom, B. S. (1984). *Taxonomy of educational objectives. Book 1/Cognitive Domain.* Boston: Allyn & Bacon.

Bowers, J., & Hatch, T. (2005). *The ASCA National Model: A framework for counseling programs* (2nd Ed.). Alexandria, VA: ASCA Publications.

Ghorpade, J., Lackritz, J., & Singh, G. (2007). Burnout and personality. *Journal of Career Assessment, 15,* 240–256.

Granello, D. H. (2000). Encouraging the cognitive development of supervisees: Using Bloom's Taxonomy in supervision. *Counselor Education and Supervision, 40,* 31–47.

Haynes, N. M., & Comer, J. P. (1993). The Yale School Development Program process, outcomes, and policy implications. *Urban Education, 28*(2), 166–199.

Hazler, R. J. (1996). *Breaking the cycle of violence: Interventions for bullying and victimization.* Washington, DC: Accelerated Development.

Henderson, A. T., & Berla, N. E. (1994). *A new generation of evidence: The family is critical to student achievement.* St. Louis, MO: Mott (C.S.) Foundation. (ERIC Document Reproduction Service No. ED375968)

Kasser, T., & Ryan, R. M. (1996). Further examining the American dream: Differential correlates of intrinsic and extrinsic goals. *Personality and Social Psychology Bulletin, 22,* 80–87.

Kunen, S., Cohen, R., & Solman, R. (1981). A levels-of-processing analysis of Bloom's Taxonomy. *Journal of Educational Psychology, 73,* 202–211.

Kuperminc, G. P., Leadbeater, B. J., Emmons, C., & Blatt, S. J. (1997). Perceived school climate and difficulties in the social adjustment of middle school students. *Applied Developmental Science, 1*, 76–88.

Learning Skills Program. (1999). Bloom's Taxonomy [Online]. Available at: http://www.coun.uvic.ca/learn/program/hndouts/bloom.html.

McGuffin, P. W. (1991). The effect of timeout duration on frequency of aggression in hospitalized children with conduct disorders. *Behavioral Residential Treatment, 6*, 279–299.

McEvoy, A., & Welker, R. (2000). Antisocial behavior, academic failure, and school climate: A critical review. *Journal of Emotional and Behavioral Disorders, 8*(3), 130–140.

McKay, M. M., Atkins, M. S., Hawkins, T., Brown, C., & Lynn, C. J. (2003). Inner-City African American parental involvement in children's schooling: Racial socialization and social support from the parent community. *American Journal of Community Psychology, 32*, 107–114.

McKenzie, J. (2003). Gambling with the children. *No Child Left, 1*(1), (2006). Available at: http://nochildleft.com/2003.jancov03.html.

Miller, G. E., & Prinz, R. J. (1990). Enhancement of social learning family interventions for childhood conduct disorders. *Psychological Bulletin, 108*(2), 291–307.

National Education Goals Panel. (1993). *The national education goals report—Volume 1: The national report.* Washington, DC: U.S. Government Printing Office.

Ryan, R. M., & Deci, E. L. (2000). Self-determination theory and the facilitation of intrinsic motivation, social development and well-being. *American Psychologist, 55*, 68–78.

Sklare, G. B. (2004). *Brief counseling that works: A solution focused approach for school counselors and administrators.* Thousand Oaks, CA: Corwin Press.

Talmon, M. (1990). *Single session therapy.* San Francisco: Jossey-Bass.

Taylor, D. L., & Tashakkori, A. (1995). Decision participation and school climate as predictors of job satisfaction and teacher's sense of efficacy. *Journal of Experimental Education, 63*(3), 217–227.

Toch, T. (1993). Violence in the schools. *U.S. News & World Report.* November 8, pp. 31–47.

U.S. Department of Education. (2006). *No Child Left Behind is working.* Retrieved June 7, 2007, from: http://www.ed.gov/nclb/overview/importance/nclbworking.html.

Index

CORWIN PRESS

The Corwin Press logo—a raven striding across an open book—represents the union of courage and learning. Corwin Press is committed to improving education for all learners by publishing books and other professional development resources for those serving the field of PreK–12 education. By providing practical, hands-on materials, Corwin Press continues to carry out the promise of its motto: **"Helping Educators Do Their Work Better."**